An OPUS book

The Character of Mind

Colin McGinn

The Character of Mind

Oxford   New York
OXFORD UNIVERSITY PRESS
1982

Oxford University Press, Walton Street, Oxford OX2 6DP

London Glasgow New York Toronto
Delhi Bombay Calcutta Madras Karachi
Kuala Lumpur Singapore Hong Kong Tokyo
Nairobi Dar es Salaam Cape Town
Melbourne Auckland

and associates in
Beirut Berlin Ibadan Mexico City Nicosia

First published as an Oxford University Press paperback 1982
and simultaneously in a hardback edition

British Library Cataloguing in Publication Data
McGinn, Colin
The character of mind. – (OPUS)
1. Mind and body   2. Intellect
I. Title   II. Series
128'.2   BD161
ISBN 0–19–219171–3
ISBN 0–19–289159–6 Pbk

Library of Congress Cataloging in Publication Data
McGinn, Colin, 1950–
The character of mind.
(OPUS)
Bibliography: p.
Includes index.
1. Psychology – Philosophy.
I. Title.   II. Series.
BF38.M39   128'.2   82–6288
ISBN 0–19–219171–3 (hard)   AACR2
ISBN 0–19–289159–6 (pbk.)

Set by Western Printing Services Ltd
Printed in Great Britain by
Richard Clay (The Chaucer Press) Ltd
Bungay, Suffolk

Preface

This book is intended as an introduction to the philosophy of mind, suitable for the general reader and beginning student. I have accordingly avoided the use of technical terms, except those whose meaning I explain as they are introduced; a dictionary should suffice for other unfamiliar words. I have not, however, sought to protect the reader from the difficulties of the subject, and there are parts of each chapter that are likely to prove taxing to the tyro; but my hope is that these will yield to concentrated attention. On many vexed issues I have written with a boldness and absence of qualification I might not allow myself elsewhere; my aim has been to give the reader something definite and stimulating to think about, rather than to present a cautious and disinterested survey of the state of the subject. But while I have tried to say something positive about the topics with which the book deals, I have made a point of accentuating the problems each topic raises; the resulting inconclusiveness is, I think, to be preferred to facile solutions or (even worse) refusals to acknowledge the difficulties.

The book contains neither the names of particular authors nor footnotes crediting the ideas discussed to their originators. I must emphasise that this is not to be taken as an indication that the views discussed have no identifiable source, still less that their source is myself. On the contrary, every page of the book shows the influence of other writers, often in the most direct way possible; I claim no especial originality for the ideas put forward, though I dare say my treatment of them has sometimes altered their original form. My excuse for this manner of composition is that to have duly cited particular authors would have greatly impeded and complicated the presentation of the material discussed, unsuiting the book for its introductory purpose. The selective bibliographies for each chapter, to be found at the end of the book, record the sources of the views dealt with, in so far as I can trace them; but it seems in order to acknowledge the main influences on each chapter here, if only in a general way. These are as follows: Chapter 2, Davidson, Nagel, Kripke, Putnam; Chapter 3, Russell; Chapter 4, Davidson, Fodor, Geach; Chapter 5, Davidson and especially O'Shaughnessy; Chapter 6, Nagel, Parfit, Shoemaker;

Epilogue, Dummett. I would also like to thank Anita Avramides for helpful critical comments and Katherine Backhouse for exemplary typing.

12 August 1981

Contents

1 Mental phenomena

Of what nature is the mind? This question identifies the philosophical topic with which we are to be concerned. But the question needs some refinement and qualification before it gives accurate expression to the range of issues with which the philosophy of mind deals. Let us start by guarding against some misleading suggestions carried by this simple way of delimiting our topic, and then proceed to clarify what sort of question it is and how we are to set about answering it.

The question 'What is the nature of the mind?' invites the retort 'Whose mind?' We do readily and commonly speak of 'the mind', but (as Aristotle warned) this is apt to confine our attentions to the *human* mind; we thus conceive our task as that of characterising the mental life of a certain terrestrial species at a certain point in its evolutionary and cultural history. But the craving for generality which typifies philosophy recommends enlarging our area of concern: we must seek an account of the mental which applies to the minds of other animals and indeed to the minds of such mentally endowed creatures as we can legitimately imagine. It is therefore better to rephrase our question by replacing 'the mind' by 'mental phenomena'. And if we keep the intended generality of the question in mind, we shall be less prone to accept accounts of the various mental phenomena which are applicable only to certain of the creatures exemplifying them; indeed it is frequently a good test of a theory of some mental phenomenon to ask whether the proposed theory would be applicable to *all* actual and possible creatures exemplifying that phenomenon. For example, we should be suspicious of the suggestion that having a pain consists in a propensity to offer certain sorts of verbal report, in the light of the consideration that creatures without language are capable of pain sensations. Similarly, but less obviously, we should question theories which make sense perception a matter of the acquisition of beliefs, in view of the point that some creatures seem capable of perceiving the world yet are hardly equipped to form *beliefs* about what they perceive. Or again, there are theories of emotion and of action which, while they seem appropriate to the case of human beings, fall down when we ask how they work for other creatures to which these concepts apply – in particular, theories that put (propositional) *thought* at the heart of those mental phenomena. We do well, then, for heuristic purposes as well as for the sake of generality, to allow our enquiry to take in minds other than the human. Perhaps the minds of all creatures will turn out, upon close examination, to be fundamentally alike, so that concentration on the human case will not misrepresent the nature of mind in general; but we should be alive to the possibility that minds may be of many kinds.

Our initial formulation of the question carries another implication which should not be taken uncritically for granted, namely that all types of mental phenomena are of the same nature. Not only may the mind of any particular kind of creature, say the human mind, have seams – in the sense that its component attributes are conceptually separable and hence could occur independently – but there may be nothing common and peculiar to all that we call mental. In other words, we should not let the initial naïve formulation of the question lull us into just assuming that the mental is a unified domain – or, as it is often put, that there is a single and universal 'criterion of the mental'. If there were no shared feature of all that we attribute to 'the mind', then the project of elucidating *the* nature of mental phenomena would be doomed to frustration – each type of mental phenomenon would have its own distinctive nature. Later we shall try to find a workable criterion of the mental and enquire whether we can do anything to level the variety with which mental phenomena present us; but we should be open to the prospect of discovering that what we commonly classify as mental has no significant unity of nature – indeed that our customary classification of various phenomena as belonging to 'the mind' is a mere historical or cultural accident. Certainly philosophers (and others) have shown less than full consensus, through the centuries, on the question of what belongs to the realm of the properly mental. Less drastically, it may turn out that the concept of mind approximates to what is sometimes called a 'family resemblance' concept, similar to the concept of a game: that is, calling a phenomenon mental is not recording the possession of some interesting single property on the part of all and only phenomena so called, but is rather a matter of drawing attention to a large number of similarities and connections which are incapable of summary capture in any simple formula. It is not – or not just – that there exists no concept, aside from the family resemblance concept in question, under which all and only instances of that concept fall; it is rather that there is no substantive or conceptually innovative necessary and sufficient condition for falling under the concept – or none that is not itself a family resemblance concept. But before we address this question as to the logical character of the concept of mind, we should say something about the status of our enquiry into the nature of mental phenomena and about the method of its prosecution.

A further defect in our original question is that it does not, as so expressed, present us with a distinctively *philosophical* field of investigation; for it says nothing to distinguish the philosophy of mind from the study of mental phenomena undertaken by scientific empirical psychology. Putting aside certain deviations in the conception of psychology adopted during its chequered history, it is surely true to say that it is the business of psychology to investigate the nature of mental phenomena – to develop theories of what these phenomena are and of the principles or laws that govern their operations. How then do the two subjects differ? Answering this question requires us to take a stand on the nature of philosophy itself – what its method is and what the status of its results – as well as on the question of how the philosophical study of mind relates to its scientific study. Some have supposed the philosophy of mind to be strictly continuous with psychology, being merely more speculative; others that it represents a primitive stage of enquiry into the mind, to be left behind when experimental methods are extended to cover areas of the mental hitherto insusceptible to properly scientific study; still others that the task of philosophy of mind is to analyse and clarify the theoretical concepts and methods employed by the science of psychology. None of these views will be adopted in this book. We get closer to the conception of the philosophy of mind adopted here by saying that we are concerned to articulate what is involved in mental *concepts*. This is not quite close enough, however; for it is a demerit of this way of describing our concern, as it is of corresponding descriptions of other areas of philosophy, that it suggests that the philosophical and the scientific studies of mind treat of different subject-matters – the latter dealing with mental phenomena themselves, the former (merely) with our concepts of them. (Still more misleading is the idea that the subject matter of philosophy of mind is mental *words*.) It is better to say that the philosopher also investigates the mental phenomena themselves but that he does so *by* investigating mental concepts: mental concepts are more the *method* of enquiry than its object. What is (or should be) meant by saying that philosophy is concerned with concepts is this: that the philosopher seeks to discover a priori necessary truths about the phenomena of mind – truths that can be ascertained without empirical study of the mind and its operations, and truths that hold good for any conceivable exemplification of the mental phenomenon in question. And such truths are to be discovered precisely by elucidating the content of our mental concepts. So the philosopher wishes to know, without being roused from his armchair, what is *essential* to the various mental phenomena; the psychologist's aim is at once more ambitious and more modest – he wants to discover by empirical means the actual workings of this or that creature's mind.

An analogy with another field may help clarify this contrast. We can pose the question 'What is the nature of language?' and mean it in two different ways. We can mean to ask after the actual grammar, phonology and so forth of particular languages (English, say), as well as to the more general question as to the properties of all human languages. These are empirical questions and their answers are not to be supposed generalisable to every conceivable language. The philosopher of language, however, has his eye on larger (if more ethereal) things: his characteristic concern is with the *essence* of language – any language – and so his procedure is to examine the concept of language with a view to discovering how any language must be. (It should be said that not all philosophers would agree with this description of their activities.) The philosopher of language is interested in the language we speak, but only as an instance of something more general – and that more general thing is to be approached by means of a conceptual enquiry. Thus the philosopher will be interested, for example, in the subject–predicate structure of English, but he will expect little or no philosophical profit from the study of irregular verbs or forms of pluralisation.

We can illustrate the above contrast, as it arises in respect of the mind, with the phenomenon of vision. The philosopher wishes to articulate the necessary and sufficient conditions for any conceivable creature to see an object, and his results are known a priori; he wants to know what it *is*, quite generally, to see something. The psychologist, on the other hand, is content to discover the workings of the actual mechanisms of vision in various sorts of organism – how, for example, human vision develops, what cues the eye exploits to produce a visual impression, how the human retina is composed. That human beings are subject to the autokinetic effect or that their retinas contain rods and cones are facts of interest to the psychologist; but they leave the philosopher of mind cold – his interest will be excited by such questions as whether it is (conceptually) possible to see an object with which one has no causal contact.

Even from these brief remarks, which await discussion of specific mental phenomena for their proper amplification, it should be plain that philosophy of mind, as here conceived, is distinct from what is sometimes called philosophy of psychology, that is, the philosophical study of the nature and significance of the results and methods of scientific psychology. This latter discipline is to the philosophy of mind as the philosophy of linguistics is to the philosophy of language, or as the philosophy of physics is to the metaphysical question as to the nature of the physical world. These fields are not of course totally unrelated, but their focus and aim are different: the former fields are second-order, needing nourishment from the sciences they depend upon; the latter are self-sustaining and are only marginally, if at all, beholden to the sciences they exist alongside of. Philosophy of mind, as it is to be pursued in this book, aims for its own kind of truths about mental phenomena and is pretty much independent (both ways) of scientific psychology; in this sense the present approach is traditional in character.

Those unfamiliar with philosophical enquiry may be forgiven for doubting whether armchair elucidation of our concepts could yield anything of intellectual substance: why should we expect to learn anything significant (or even true!) from reflecting upon our ordinary concepts? This worry is in a way entirely reasonable – for surely it is not *generally* true that our concepts contain enough to surprise or interest the enquiring intellect. But only certain concepts are deemed to be of philosophical interest – those with the richness and depth to reveal something significant about the phenomena to which they apply. Thus we do not expect that the essential nature of animal species or chemical substances or physical changes will be disclosed to us merely be reflecting upon the ordinary concepts of (say) *cat*, *salt* or *freezing*: we acknowledge that scientific investigation is needed to reveal the essential nature of these things. Why, it is reasonable to ask, should the matter stand differently with respect to the concepts of *pain*, *belief*, *action*, *person*? If the case is indeed different with these mental concepts, then that should really strike us as a significant fact – more, as a clue to the special nature of the mind, as seen through the concepts that characterise it. And that we can do interesting philosophy of mind at all shows something important about mental concepts and hence mental phenomena. What it shows is that the essence of mental phenomena is contained a priori in mental concepts: that is to say, mental concepts have a depth and suggestiveness that makes it possible and fruitful (as we shall see) to conduct a philosophical investigation of their content. (Whether *any* concept which admits of such philosophical investigation is either mental or somehow intimately bound up with the mind is an interesting question, bearing upon whether the a priori knowledge we have in these areas is connected with the special access we have to our own minds. But, fortunately, we need not take up that large question now, since the present claim is only that *if* a concept is mental then it will be susceptible of philosophical articulation.) It is thus precisely because mental concepts have this depth and translucency that philosophy of mind can be a substantive field distinct from psychology. By contrast, there can be no philosophy of chemicals independent of the science of chemistry.

The task of elucidating mental concepts involves a special difficulty, not common to all concepts in which philosophers interest themselves. Mental concepts are unique in that they are ascribed in two, seemingly very different, sorts of circumstances: we apply them to ourselves on the strength of our 'inner' awareness of our mental states, as when a person judges of himself that he has a headache; and we also apply them to others on the strength of their 'outer' manifestations in behaviour and speech. These two ways of ascribing mental concepts are referred to as first-person and third-person ascriptions, after the grammatical form of their typical expression. The special difficulty presented by these two modes of ascription is that it is clearly the same concepts that are ascribed in first- and third-person judgements, yet there is a strong and natural tendency to suppose that the content of mental concepts reflects their characteristic conditions of ascription. We thus appear forced to choose from among three unattractive positions as to the content of these concepts: either (i) we favour the first-person uses and so encounter difficulty in giving a satisfactory account of how mental concepts are applied to others; or (ii) we favour third-person uses and so omit to register the special character of our first-person ascriptions; or (iii) we try to combine both uses, thus producing a sort of hybrid or amalgam of two apparently unrelated elements. The problem arises because we cannot plausibly sever the meaning of a mental word (content of a mental concept) from the conditions under which we know it to be satisfied, yet these seem utterly different in the first- and third-person cases, and so the concepts are pulled in two directions at once. Historically, views of the mind can be classified according to which direction they have allowed themselves to be pulled in: either claiming the essential nature of mental phenomena to be revealed only from the perspective of the subject exemplifying them ('Cartesianism'); or claiming that the real nature of the mental is shown only in our judgements about the states of mind of others ('behaviourism'). Both views give mental concepts a unitary content, but both seem irremediably partial in their account of that content. According to which perspective you take up in reflecting upon some mental phenomenon you arrive at a certain view about the very nature of that phenomenon. It would be fine if we could somehow, as theorists, prescind from both perspectives and just contemplate how mental phenomena are, so to say, in themselves; but this is precisely what seems conceptually unfeasible, because of the constitutive connections of mental concepts with the conditions under which they are known to be satisfied. To avoid the three unattractive alternatives – Cartesianism, behaviourism, an amalgam of the two – we seem to need the idea of a single mental reality somehow neutral between the first- and third-person perspectives; the problem is that there does not appear to be any such idea – we cannot *first* fashion a conception of the mind and *then* go on to specify the ways in which the mind is known. In a word, there is no epistemologically neutral conception of the mind: we cannot form an idea of *what* some mental phenomenon is without adopting one or other epistemological perspective on it. In this predicament the difficulty of doing justice to both aspects of mental concepts is inherent in the topic, and is not to be dismissed as a mere confusion of thought. Since the epistemology of mind is constitutive of its nature, and since the epistemology is thus divided between first- and third-person ascriptions, it seems that the only way to find some unity in our mental concepts is to treat one or other perspective as primary in relation to the other – to regard one perspective as better revealing the true nature of the mental phenomenon in question. The hope, then, is to find a plausible way to connect the concept so determined with the other secondary aspect of its content. There is, furthermore, no very good reason to suppose that all mental concepts will have their primary content given from the same perspective: if mental phenomena are not uniform in nature, then it is possible that some will be better apprehended from the first-person perspective, some from the third-person. The best advice to follow in practice is just to ask yourself, with respect to a given mental concept, whether justice has been done to both perspectives, and to be aware of which perspective is primarily shaping your conception of the mental phenomenon in question. There is probably no uniform way of resolving the tension generated by the two perspectives, indeed no way of completely resolving it in any particular case. This peculiarity of the philosophy of mind may in fact place a permanent obstacle in the way of arriving at a theoretically satisfying conception of the mind.

With these abstract matters of method duly noted, let us now descend into the realm of the mental and attempt some sort of preliminary classification or taxonomy of what we find there. When we have divided up the territory we can return to the question whether there is anything each type of mental phenomenon has in common with all other types. Many schemes of classification have been suggested, each with its merits and demerits; the scheme that we will find most useful in what follows divides mental phenomena into what we can call *sensations* and *propositional attitudes*. By sensations we shall mean bodily feelings like pains, tickles, nausea, as well as perceptual experiences like seeming to see a red pillar-box, hearing a loud trumpet, tasting a sweet strawberry. These differ in an important respect, which calls for a subdivision within the class of what we are calling sensations: bodily sensations do not have an intentional object in the way perceptual experiences do. We distinguish between a visual experience and what it is an experience of; but we do not make this distinction in respect of pains. Or again, visual experiences represent the world as being a certain way, but pains have no such representational content. Grammatically, perceptual verbs are transitive; words for bodily sensations are adjectival. Nevertheless, there is a point in classifying them together, because they are both defined by their phenomenology, that is, by how they *seem* to the subject. They both have what is sometimes called 'qualitative content'. It is natural to say that what it is to undergo a sensation, in this broad sense, is a matter of what it is *like* for the subject of the sensation. The second main category consists of those mental phenomena which have propositional content, that is, the ascription of which involves the use of a 'that'-clause, as in 'Jones believes that the sky is blue.' This class of propositional attitudes itself has important subdivisions, as significant for some purposes as the fact that they are all endowed with propositional content. Thus we are to include not only cognitive states like belief but also conative and affective attitudes – for example, desiring or intending that you get an apple, and fearing that you will be run over. A propositional attitude, of any of these kinds, is identified by two factors: the type of attitude it is – believing, hoping, fearing, intending etc. – and the proposition on to which the attitude is directed. We are not inclined to suppose that propositional attitudes are, like sensations, defined by a distinctive phenomenology. This difference affords an illustration of the way in which our conception of different mental phenomena can be dominated by either the first- or third-person perspectives. In the case of sensations we seem to be taking up the first-person perspective, considering what it is like for the subject of the sensation and ignoring, or regarding as secondary, how a person's sensations are presented to others. In the case of propositional attitudes it seems more natural to accord central importance to how the attitude figures in shaping a person's propensities to act; the dispositional properties of propositional attitudes seem integral to their nature. In neither case can we wholly eliminate the contribution of the less dominant perspective, but the nature of the phenomena directs us to regard different perspectives as primary in respect of the two mental categories.

This twofold classification is not exclusive in the sense that any given mental state has just one of these characteristics. Consider seeing that it is sunny or being terrified that you will be called upon to make the speech: these mental states have both sensational and propositional aspects, and so are identified both phenomenologically and by way of the propositions to which they are related. About such mental states we might say two things apropos of the suggested taxonomy: we might claim that they are really compound mental states, made up of a sensation and a propositional attitude in combination, and that the taxonomy should be applied at the non-compound level; or we might say that the taxonomy classifies mental *features*, not mental states as we find them – and in the above cases we have to do with the two sorts of feature exemplified in a single mental state. Either way the taxonomy retains its usefulness.

Sensations have the look of something simpler, more primitive, than propositional attitudes. Sensations are present in animals not really up to propositional thought, and babies evidently feel things before they begin to think things. Sensations seem to belong to an earlier and more primitive stage of evolution and individual development; propositional attitudes are to be seen as superimposed upon a prior basis of sensation. Sensations are pre-rational in the sense that their enjoyment is not sufficient to qualify a creature as a rational agent, whereas the onset of propositional mental states is coeval with the introduction of rationality. When we attribute beliefs and desires to a creature we are in the business of making rational sense of its doings; but attributing sensations does not involve us in making *sense* – in this sense – of anything. When we explain a person's behaviour by attributing propositional attitudes to the person we represent the behaviour as rational from the person's point of view (that is, his set of beliefs and desires); but when we explain behaviour by ascribing sensations to a creature we are not yet in the realm of explanation by *reasons* but are merely exhibiting a pattern of (non-rational) cause and effect. As a consequence, the need to represent a creature's propositional attitudes as rationally related one to another, the whole forming a (relatively) coherent web, has no real analogue in the ascription of sensations: there is nothing like propositional content to confer logical relations between sensations, and hence no normative constraint shaping the pattern of sensations a creature may exemplify. The question of the rationality of a sensation does not arise.

Further differences between sensations and propositional attitudes emerge when we consider how the notion of *consciousness* applies in the two cases. We can come at this question by asking how the idea of the unconscious is to be applied to the two sorts of mental phenomena; and here we immediately notice a striking asymmetry between the cases. Common sense recognises, and Freud drove the point home, that propositional attitudes may be unconscious: we may be unaware of the beliefs and desires that influence our actions and conscious life – we may indeed be quite incapable, save in special circumstances, of becoming aware of these. For this reason there is no contradiction or incoherence in the idea of a propositional attitude which *never* reaches consciousness. And this suggests that the property of being conscious is something superadded to a propositional attitude; it does not belong intrinsically to a belief that it be a conscious belief. But the case seems otherwise with sensations; we cannot conceive of them as existing in a state of unconsciousness, with consciousness as an extrinsic property only contingently satisfied. This is simply because to have (say) a pain is to feel a pain, and a felt pain precisely is a conscious pain. Of course there is the odd phenomenon of, as we say, not noticing a pain one nevertheless has; but what a strict parallel with propositional attitudes requires is the possibility of someone having an intense and terrible pain throughout his life and yet never being conscious of it – and this appears unintelligible. If a sensation departs from consciousness, we suppose it to go thereby out of existence; but not so with propositional attitudes. This difference needs to be explained, and it prompts the suspicion that what it is for the two sorts of mental phenomena to be conscious may not be the same. The difference also bears out the intuition, mentioned earlier, that different epistemological perspectives are appropriate to conceiving sensations and propositional attitudes: for if the latter mental states are not intrinsically conscious, then we cannot take the first-person perspective to be constitutive of their nature, since in ascribing unconscious beliefs or desires to oneself one is in essentially the same epistemological situation as he who ascribes those states to one. Since our conception of the intrinsic nature of propositional attitudes is not sensitive to whether they are conscious or unconscious, we find it natural to take up a third-person perspective on them; but because sensations cannot be unconscious we naturally take what is distinctive and definitive of them to be the manner of their presentation in the first-person case.

We said that consciousness is intrinsic to sensations but extrinsic to propositional attitudes: to have a sensation is to have it consciously, whereas the presence of propositional attitudes is not sufficient for them to be conscious. What needs to be added to the mere presence of the latter to render them conscious? It does not seem right to suppose that we need to add a phenomenology – a way it seems to the person to have the propositional attitude in question – for we saw that these mental states are not defined by what it is like to have them. Nor is it at all clear what it would be to add a phenomenology to a mental state – certainly we cannot make sense of that idea in respect of sensations. So it does not seem correct to regard the consciousness of propositional attitudes as the same *sort* of thing as the consciousness of sensations. This suspicion is reinforced by the consideration that it seems to be a necessary condition (and arguably a sufficient one) of a belief being conscious that one believe oneself to have that belief, that is, that one have a second-order belief; but this is not plausible for sensations, since it seems possible to have sensations, and *eo ipso* have them consciously, and not be capable of beliefs of any kind, let alone second-order beliefs – think of simple sentient organisms. If these reflections are on the right track, then the notion of consciousness is not univocal in application to the two sorts of mental phenomena; so again our taxonomy corresponds to real differences among mental phenomena.

The conclusion just reached bears critically on the question whether it is possible to devise or discover a criterion of the mental, a feature common and peculiar to mental phenomena. It bears on this question because the most promising candidate for such a criterion invokes consciousness as the touchstone of what is of the mind. This criterion needs careful formulation, since we have already acknowledged that some mental states can be unconscious. One way of preserving the consciousness criterion in the face of this point is to say, not that a state of a person is mental if and only if it *is* conscious, but rather if and only if it *could* be conscious. This is nearer the mark, but there is the question what is the force of the 'could'. We want to allow that a person may be psychologically incapable of bringing the contents of his unconscious to consciousness, and that this incapacity may be as radical as you wish. In view of this we do better to weaken the connection with consciousness still further while not severing it altogether: let us then say that a state is mental if and only if it is *of the same kind* as states which *are* conscious. Thus an unconscious belief, even a necessarily unconscious belief, rates as a part of the mind because it is the same kind of state – namely, a belief state – as states which simply are conscious. This criterion uses the idea of consciousness essentially yet allows room for the radically unconscious. However, even if this criterion is roughly correct it is unclear whether it provides exactly what we sought, namely a single differentiating property of all that is mental. For, first, the criterion scarcely rates as a surprising piece of conceptual analysis; it sounds a bit too much like saying that games are distinguished by the fact that they are activities which are *played* – the analysis seems too close to what it is meant to analyse. And, second, it resembles the case of games and playing in another way, in that the concept of consciousness, like the concept of playing, is itself a family resemblance concept (although the family has only two members). That is, since the notion of consciousness is not univocal – it consists in different things in different cases (compare playing) – we have not really supplied a single common property satisfied by all varieties of mental phenomena. We cannot think of consciousness as a homogeneous property – like being red or straight – shared by all mental phenomena which have it; our classification into the mental and the non-mental must then rest upon a looser basis of similarities and connections, as does our division of activities into games and non-games. (What is not, however, as clear as we might wish is whether our habit of dividing the mind from the rest of the world really reflects a genuine division in nature and not just an accident of convention or intellectual history. The less iconoclastic position is to be preferred, but a vulnerability to the iconoclast should be admitted.) Perhaps the concept of mind resembles the concept of *life* in this respect: we do pretty confidently divide the world into the living and the non-living, but we are hard put to it to produce any but a trivial specification of what enables us to effect this division. We can, of course, say that something is living just if it is *animate*; but this is too close to mere synonymy to be informative, and besides exhibits the same sort of (quasi-)family resemblance character as the concept it is supposed to define.

We might hope to fill out and fortify our criterion of the mental by giving an account of what consciousness *is*. One way of doing this is to ask how we would set about conveying what it is to be conscious to someone who lacked this concept. However, this looks like a hopeless enterprise, because the notion of consciousness seems available only to those who already know what it is to be conscious by virtue of being conscious: that is, if you are conscious you know what it is to be so (if you are capable of knowledge at all); but if you are not you will never learn. Consciousness, like redness or sweetness, belongs to that range of properties that can be grasped only by direct acquaintance: just as a man born blind cannot really know what it is to be red, so a being without consciousness cannot be taught what it is to be conscious – and not because, not being conscious, he cannot be taught anything. And concepts which can be grasped only through acquaintance with what they are concepts of are, by definition, concepts we cannot hope to explain in a non-circular manner. But there is, compounding the ineffability, a way in which consciousness is elusive even to acquaintance, as an exercise in introspection will reveal. Consider your consciousness *of* some item – an external object, your own body, a sensation – and try to focus attention on that relation: as many philosophers have observed, this relation of consciousness to its objects is peculiarly impalpable and diaphanous – all you come across in introspection are the objects of consciousness, not consciousness itself. This feature of consciousness has induced some thinkers to describe consciousness as a kind of inner emptiness; it is nothing *per se* but a pure directedness on to things other than itself. No wonder then that it is hard to say what consciousness intrinsically is.

There is, though, something instructive that we can say about the nature of consciousness – and this is that the possession of consciousness is not a matter of *degree*. Put differently, the concept of consciousness does not permit us to conceive of genuinely borderline cases of sentience, cases in which it is inherently indeterminate whether a creature is conscious: either a creature definitely is conscious or it is definitely not. Note that this is a claim about what it is to *be* conscious, not a claim about our *knowledge* as to whether a creature is conscious. There can certainly be cases where we are not *sure* whether a creature is conscious, so that our ascription of conscious states will be tentative; but this is irrelevant to the question whether, *if* the creature is conscious, this can be a matter of degree. To see this, suppose you know all the facts about a creature: could all the facts leave it indeterminate whether the creature is conscious? We could know all the facts about the colour of some object and yet admit that it is inherently indeterminate *which* colour the object is, since we allow that there can be borderline cases of (say) blue; but it does not seem that a parallel situation could obtain in respect of consciousness. Thus we can make no sense of the possibility that a state of a creature might be a borderline case of sensation, precisely because sensations are necessarily conscious. The case is somewhat different for propositional attitudes: it seems less than evident that there cannot be borderline cases of belief, as perhaps with certain animals; but this is because beliefs are not necessarily conscious – and borderline cases of belief will not be borderline cases of *conscious* belief. If consciousness is an all-or-nothing matter, then it follows that the possession of a mind is also an all-or-nothing matter, since consciousness is what characterises the mind. There may be many kinds of mind, but none of these is a case where it is inherently indeterminate whether there is mind or not.

The concept of mind contrasts in this respect with the concept of life, for it is not difficult to persuade oneself that the latter concept does admit of borderline cases. Our concept of the living is vague enough to allow us to envisage the possibility of things about which it is simply not determinate whether they are living – think of bacteria and various kinds of organic molecule. But in the case of consciousness its possession is a matter of there being something 'inner', some way the world appears *to* the creature; and we cannot imagine the position of a creature for whom it is indeterminate whether there is such an 'inner' subjective aspect. This contrast between life and mind is made especially vivid by considering the genesis of these properties in evolution. In the case of life we have to do with a gradual transition from the plainly inanimate to the indisputably living; but in the case of consciousness we cannot take such a gradualist view, admitting the existence of intermediate stages. The emergence of consciousness must rather be compared to a sudden switching on of a light, narrow as the original shaft must have been. According to this thesis about consciousness, we conceive the minds of lowly creatures as consisting in (so to speak) a small speck of consciousness quite definitely possessed, not in the partial possession of something admitting of degrees. Perhaps this feature of consciousness is connected with the apparent *simplicity* of consciousness; for if consciousness is a simple quality it cannot be made up of constituents whose separation might produce borderline cases. Or perhaps it is because consciousness is so different from the merely material that nothing could count as an instance of something intermediate between them – a consideration that does not apply to life. Whatever the explanation is – whether indeed the all-or-nothing character of consciousness can be explained – this seems to be a feature that any account of consciousness must respect. And there are theories of the mind, such as materialism and behaviourism, that will find this feature problematic, since the concepts in terms of which they choose to explain mental phenomena do not themselves exhibit this all-or-nothing character. It is therefore in place to ask, of any theory of the mind, whether it can accommodate this feature of consciousness – and if it cannot, what view it takes of the intuition that consciousness is so constituted.

We may summarise this chapter as follows: the aim of the philosophy of mind is to conduct an a priori investigation into the essential nature of mental phenomena, by elucidating the latent content of mental concepts; mental phenomena can be approached from a first-person or a third-person perspective, both of which need to be integrated (if this be possible) into a unitary account; these phenomena may usefully be divided into sensations and propositional attitudes, which differ in their nature; both classes of mental phenomena are intimately bound up with consciousness, though not in the same way; consciousness itself is known only by acquaintance, is diaphanous, and is not a matter of degree. With these preliminaries to hand we can now turn to discuss some of the problems surrounding the nature of mind.

2 Mind and body

The question as to the relation between mental phenomena and physical states of the body, specifically of the brain, is generally referred to as 'the mind–body problem'. There is a reason for calling the question of the nature of this relation a *problem*, which may be put as follows. When we think reflectively of mental phenomena we find that we acknowledge them to possess two sets of properties: one set which invites us to distinguish the mental realm from the physical, the other which firmly locates the mental within the physical world. Among the first set of properties are subjectivity, infallible first-person knowledge, consciousness, meaning, rationality, freedom and self-awareness. These properties are not to be found in the world of mere matter, and so lead us to suppose the mind to be set apart from the physical body: we seem compelled to accord a *sui generis* mode of reality to mental phenomena. The simplest expression of this conviction that the mind must be distinguished from the body is the feeling that a pain or a thought could not really just *be* a mere arrangement of molecules, of whatever degree of complexity. That which pertains to consciousness seems just different in nature from any physical facts about a person's body. Yet, on the other hand, we have to reckon with another set of truths about the mental, apparently pushing us in the opposite direction: mental phenomena cannot be conceived as quite *outside* the physical world, as abstract entities such as numbers have been supposed to be, enjoying no commerce with mere matter. Thus we equally recognise the following truths: that the mind has some sort of spatio-temporal location, roughly where the body is; that each mind has a characteristic mode of embodiment determined by its capacities to perceive and act – indeed that the notion of a disembodied mind is (to say the least) of dubious coherence; that there are causal connections of many kinds between mental events and physical events; that the brain, itself a physical organ of the body, is intimately related to mental activity, its integrity and functioning necessary to the integrity and functioning of the mind; that mental phenomena seem to emerge, both in evolution and individual development, from a basis of matter organised in physically explicable ways. These considerations incline us to regard the mind as *somehow* physical in nature, since it is natural to suppose that only what is itself physical could be so enmeshed in the physical world.

It is impossible not to be impressed with the applicability of both sets of properties to the mind, and to admit that both must find a place in any account of the relation between mind and body. The problem is that the two sets of truths seem to be in fundamental tension, since one set makes us think the mind *could* not be physical while the other tells us that it *must* be. It is this tension that makes it appropriate to speak of the mind–body *problem*. (Notice that the problem of mind and body is not the prerogative of man; it arises also for other animals. And it helps, in freeing our thoughts of prejudice and ideology, to consider the problem in application to minds other than our own: nothing essential will be lost if we take rats or monkeys or Martians as exemplars of the problem.)

A satisfying solution to the problem would allow us to acknowledge both sets of truths about the mental by relieving the tension between them. Simply repudiating outright one set or the other would also relieve the tension, but at an intolerable cost. In practice, suggested solutions have tended to be pulled in one direction or the other, according to how impressed their authors have been with one or the other set of properties; they have then tried to do justice to the aspects of the mental deemed secondary, generally without producing full conviction. As is typical in philosophy, we are here confronted by a conceptual conflict which cannot be easily resolved in a way that does justice to all the conflicting considerations. Thus, on the one hand, various brands of *dualism* are offered as metaphysical expressions of the idea that the mind is different in essential nature from the body: mind and body are conceived as distinct things or substances, more or less tenuously related. On the other hand, there are versions of *monism*, holding that there is only matter and its material attributes, mind being a particular kind of arrangement of the material world. Predictably enough, dualism is driven to desperate expedients in endeavouring to relate the mind back to the physical world from which it has been extruded; while monism is forced to deny or distort the distinctive characteristics of the mind. Let us review some of the more instructive defects of traditional dualism and monism, hoping thereby to edge nearer to a position which combines their attractions while avoiding their difficulties; we shall, however, find that this is no easy task. We begin with monism.

The clearest and most uncompromising version of monism is the thesis that mental phenomena are literally identical with physical phenomena: if a person has a sensation or a thought and a neurophysiologist is examining the relevant portions of his brain, then the mental state is nothing other than the physical state thus observed. Moreover, whenever a mental state of that type occurs in a creature's mind there is the same type of physical state in the brain, these being identical. This sort of monism is sometimes called the *type*-identity theory. The model for such type identities is said to be provided by such theoretical identifications as that of water with H_2O or heat with molecular motion: just as we may be presented with one and the same phenomenon in two different ways and subsequently discover the identity, so – it has been claimed – we may be presented in two different ways with a mental phenomenon, physically and (more familiarly) mentally. An analogy would be this: a substance, such as water, may present quite different appearances when looked at with the naked eye and when examined with a microscope, so that it will not be obvious that it is one and the same thing that is thus presented. Similarly, it is said that pain may appear in one way to you who are enduring it and in another to the brain scientist examining your grey matter – yet the same thing is being presented. To make sense of these cases of discovered identities we need a distinction between the *property* denoted by a word and the *concept* it expresses: we can then say that 'water' and 'H_2O' denote the same property (the same *type*) yet do not express the same concept (have the same meaning). Properties are what get identified; concepts are what make the identification empirical and informative. Thus it is claimed that 'pain' and 'C-fibre stimulation' may denote the same property although they express different concepts. And just as H_2O constitutes the nature of water according to modern chemistry, though this is not derivable from the concept of water, so C-fibre stimulation may constitute the nature of pain according to modern neurophysiology, though this is not contained in the concept of pain. What this type-identity theory attempts to do is to account for the physical involvements of mental phenomena by identifying mental properties with physical properties, while at the same time allowing room for (at least some) of the distinctive features of mind by keeping mental and physical concepts distinct. This is an appealing and ingenious idea; but can we really conceive the relation between mental properties and mental concepts on the model of the water and heat cases?

There are a number of closely related difficulties in any such view, which seem to have a common source. It is not that there is some general problem with the idea of distinct concepts picking out the same property; indeed this is precisely what is wanted to describe what is going on in the uncontentious cases of theoretical identification. It is rather that mental concepts are intuitively such that no physical concept *could* characterise the essential nature of the mental property denoted. In other words, it seems that mental concepts *already* contain the essence of mental phenomena and that physical concepts are necessarily unsuited to this role; whereas, by contrast, it seems implicit in our ordinary concepts of physical substances, for example, the concept of water, that they do *not* already contain the essential nature of the substances they denote but rather leave a gap into which a scientific characterisation of the substance is to be slotted. The former concepts close off what the latter leave open.

As we should expect, the essence-specifying character of mental concepts is tied to their epistemology: that is, how mental phenomena are presented from the first- and third-person perspectives determines their nature as revealed in the concepts applied from those perspectives. Thus from the first-person perspective the fact of consciousness is what informs our conception of the nature of mental states; and it is consciousness which seems incapable of possessing a physical nature. From the third-person perspective our conception of mental states is informed by the behavioural criteria we use to apply mental concepts to others; and criterial patterns of behaviour seem equally incapable, though for different reasons, of having a physical essence in the brain – they are too loosely connected with states of the brain for that to be feasible. As we remarked in Chapter 1, the first-person perspective is more integral to sensations than to propositional attitudes, so this perspective will dominate in fixing our conception of the nature of sensations: their subjective phenomenological nature is what blocks identification with the physical, since the physical world does not possess this feature of first-person subjectivity – it is purely objective in nature. In the case of propositional attitudes, the third-person perspective is at least as important as the first-person perspective in shaping our conception of these mental states. Thus it is natural to look to their ascription to others for the ground of their irreducibility to the physical; and here we find principles governing their ascription, and hence (partially) definitive of their nature, which are inapplicable to physical states of the body. The principles in question concern the connection between the possession of propositional attitudes and the notion of rationality: in our ascription of propositional mental states we must always attend to the logical relations that hold among the attitudes ascribed, and so propositional attitude ascriptions are (partly) controlled by various *normative* considerations – that is, considerations about what attitudes the person *ought* to have, given that he has others. So in describing someone psychologically we must conform our ascriptions to certain canons of rationality, or else we will not be making sense of the person: without some measure of conformity to normative considerations we shall not be able to find the person rationally intelligible. These principles, implicit in all our thoughts about the thoughts of others, are peculiar to the mental realm; our ascription of physical states to a person's body and brain needs no sensitivity to principles governing what physical states the person *ought* (rationally) to be in given that he is in certain other physical states. So it seems that propositional attitudes, by virtue of their constitutive involvement in the normative, are not the *sort* of state whose nature could be given in terms of physical states, in view of the indifference of the physical to the normative.

The manner in which normative considerations operate from the third-person point of view is mirrored in a certain way from the first-person perspective, and this brings out a connection between rationality and self-consciousness. A person adjusts his beliefs (and sometimes his desires) under two sorts of pressure: the impact of new information which confirms or disconfirms the beliefs he already holds; and by noticing inconsistencies, of a logical nature, between the beliefs he already possesses. Since a person is not simultaneously aware of all his beliefs, it is perfectly possible – indeed commonplace – that conflicts among beliefs go unnoticed; it is thus possible to believe something as well as believing its opposite, precisely through lack of omniscience about what you believe. But once such a conflict comes to awareness one or the other belief must go – normative considerations then operate to determine your beliefs. What is notable is that normative principles influence your beliefs in the most obvious and decisive way when you become *aware of* your beliefs and hence of their inconsistency. If a person were not aware of his beliefs, then he could not be aware of their inconsistency; but awareness of inconsistency is (primarily) what allows normative considerations to get purchase on beliefs; so the rational adjustment of beliefs one to another seems to involve self-consciousness, that is, knowledge of what you believe. Without such self-consciousness the control of logic over thought would be deprived of its compelling force; rationality as we know it requires knowledge of the contents of one's own mind. We might find some small corroboration of this point in the irrational ways of the Freudian unconscious: perhaps unconscious thoughts tolerate more illogic in their interrelations than conscious thoughts because they are not similarly subjected to the normative scrutiny consciousness brings – knowledge of one's attitudes breeds intolerance of their irrationality. We might then see the adherence to normative considerations in the third-person case as presupposing an ascription of self-consciousness to the subject of the attitude ascriptions thus normatively controlled: we try to find the other rational because we assume him to be a self-conscious appraiser of his own rationality.

These reflections on propositional attitudes, rationality and self-consciousness encourage a further thesis, namely that the very possession of propositional attitudes requires self-consciousness: for the possession of propositional attitudes requires sensitivity to principles of rationality, and such sensitivity in turn depends upon awareness of one's attitudes. It follows from this thesis that there cannot be creatures with propositional attitudes which lack self-consciousness – a claim we might well find independently plausible. Thoughts (and the like) are indeed a sophisticated accomplishment, not granted to all creatures possessed of minds, that is, capable of sensations. And note that there is no parallel argument connecting sensational mental phenomena with self-consciousness: sensations are not subject to normative considerations, and so do not in the same way point us in the direction of self-consciousness. This asymmetry between sensations and propositional attitudes in respect of self-consciousness thus seems intuitively acceptable; and we have an *explanation* of it once we connect rationality with self-consciousness. What we also have is a link between the constitutive principles that prevent the reductive identification of propositional attitudes with brain states, that is, the principles of rationality, and the phenomenon of consciousness. Consciousness thus appears to be at the root of the physical irreducibility of both sensations and propositional attitudes.

The thesis that mental concepts do not determine properties with a physical nature naturally leads to the claim that mental and physical types are not *necessarily* correlated; indeed the latter claim, if correct, can be construed as an argument for the former thesis. This is because an identification of properties is not compatible with the possibility that they be independently instantiated. Thus suppose we find pain to be correlated in human beings with C-fibre stimulation: if this correlation is merely contingent, so that it is possible to have one of the correlated items without the other, then they cannot be identical. And it does *seem* that a creature *could* have pain and not C-fibre stimulation: pain might be correlated with some other kind of physical state in that creature. (The converse possibility, C-fibre stimulation without pain, is harder to assess; we shall return to it.) Quite generally, with respect to any mental attribute it seems possible for different creatures to possess the attribute and yet differ in what sort of brain state correlates with the attribute. So the connection between mental state and correlated brain state cannot be so intimate as to warrant calling the latter the *nature* of the former, in the way that H_2O may be said to constitute the nature of water. This is not to say that mental states are only contingently embodied or that they may be exemplified in the absence of *any* physical correlates; it is just to make the more modest – but still damaging to type-monism – claim that there is no *unique* physical basis for any given mental type.

The purport of this claim may be seen from a comparison with what we want to say about computer programmes and the physical hardware in which they are exemplified. In order for a computer programme to run it needs to be 'embodied' in the physical hardware of an appropriate machine; but the nature of the programme itself leaves open what sort of hardware may embody it – and so the same programme may be run on different sorts of machine. But this analogy, though it brings out the modesty of the contingency thesis in respect of mental and physical properties, should not be immediately taken to demonstrate that mental concepts and computer concepts are concepts of the same kind – specifically, that the mind is to be compared to a computer programme. This plainly does not follow from the fact that both are only contingently connected with physical properties, and indeed brief reflection indicates that the source of the contingency is different in the two cases. In the mental case it was consciousness that seemed to render monism implausible: since consciousness could not have a physical essence, we can conceive of conscious states being associated with different bodily conditions. But in the computer case this is not the ground of the contingency; it seems rather to be the *abstractness* of computer programmes that gives them a non-physical nature. Mental states do not seem similarly abstract, and so the source of their irreducibility to the physical is quite different from that of the physical irreducibility of computer programmes. Nevertheless the analogy between abstract states and conscious states is instructive; it helps us to see that it can be true a priori that a range of properties is necessarily not capturable in purely physical terms – and so to appreciate the difficulties of monism better.

The shortcomings of type-monism make it tempting to resort to dualism. Dualism is the doctrine that mental phenomena inhere in an immaterial substance which is utterly distinct from the material substance composing the body: just as physical states are qualifications of a certain kind of stuff, namely matter, so mental states are qualifications of a different kind of stuff, incorporeal in nature. This doctrine can seem attractive because it takes with the utmost seriousness the idea that mind is essentially different from matter, to the extent of introducing a special sort of substance to constitute the nature of the mental: the hope is that if we locate mind in a specially fashioned stuff we shall be able to do justice to, perhaps even explain, the distinctive features of the mental. There are, however, at least three classes of objection to the dualist theory, which are formidable enough to remove its apparent attractiveness.

First, the idea of a peculiarly mental substance is, when you think about it, extremely weird: it is quite unclear that there is any intelligible conception associated with the words 'immaterial substance'. This is shown in the fact that the alleged substance tends to get characterised purely negatively; it is simply a kind of substance that is *not* material. But we need some more positive description of what it is if we are to be convinced that we are speaking of anything comprehensible. In fact, we are prone, in trying to form a coherent conception of the alleged immaterial substance, to picture it in imagination as an especially ethereal or attenuated kind of matter, stuff of the rarefied sort we imagine (with dubious coherence) the bodies of ghosts to be made from – the kind of stuff through which a hand could pass without disturbance. In so far as the idea of immaterial substance gains content from such excesses of imagination, it is mere fancy and not to be received as sober metaphysics. The strangeness of the idea comes out in the difficulty the dualist has in coping with such questions as whether immaterial substances are located in space, or whether there could be a science, analogous to the science of matter, investigating the laws and inner workings of the incorporeal stuff. If it is not located in space, then how do mental phenomena manage to interact with things which are so located? But if it is located, then how is this possible without the possession of properties of extension, mass, gravitational force etc.? And what would a science of immaterial substance look like? What sorts of concepts would it use? Would it represent its subject-matter as particulate or continuous in structure? Would it yield quantitative laws characterising special sorts of non-physical forces? We do not really know how to start answering such questions, and good sense counsels us not to put ourselves into the embarrassing position of having to take them seriously.

Second, there is a real doubt as to whether, even if we could make sense of it, the immaterial substance is capable of discharging the role it was introduced to play. Indeed, it is arguable that it is only our incapacity to form a clear idea of such a substance that induces us to suppose that locating mental phenomena in it is any advance on monism. The properties of the immaterial substance are supposed to constitute the nature of mental states: but what sorts of property are these? Here we seem faced with a dilemma: either we award the immaterial substance properties beyond the familiar mental properties, or we do not. If we do, thus conjecturing the existence of properties of mind hitherto undiscovered, then we seem to have the old problems of monism in a new form, since there will still be the question how *these* properties can constitute the essential nature of sensations and propositional attitudes. We cannot, without absurdity, postulate the existence of *other* conscious states which constitute the nature of the familiar ones; but it seems that nothing else can be the essence of our conscious states. The problem for immaterial substance is thus fundamentally the same as the problem of giving consciousness a material nature, namely that we are trying to explain consciousness in terms of what is not conscious: the trouble was that we cannot capture what is inner and subjective in terms of properties that are neither of these. On the other hand, if we deny that the immaterial substance has properties beyond the familiar mental properties, then the hypothesis of dualism begins to look empty: we are reduced to the claim that there is nothing more to be said about the immaterial substance than that it is the locus of sensations and propositional attitudes – we have no independent conception of its nature. But this seems to amount to the triviality that we have the mental states we have; it does not provide a metaphysical account of what our having those states consists in.

But third, and most powerfully, dualism has the problem of explaining how the mind is related to the body and to the physical world at large; the price of locating the mind in an immaterial realm is that it becomes sealed off from the physical world in which we know it to be enmeshed. The dependence of mind on brain thus becomes a mystery. Why does injury to the brain impair mental functions? Why is there a systematic correspondence between the structure of different creatures' brains and the sort of minds they have? Why do we need a complex brain at all if the mind is located in its own substance with its own principles of operation? On the dualist hypothesis all that would be needed in the way of physical hardware is some sort of conduit linking occurrences in the mental and physical worlds; the complexity of the brain as we find it then looks like excess machinery. Moreover, embodiment itself comes to seem merely fortuitous, because mental phenomena are held to reside in a separate non-bodily substance. Thus, if the mind is distinct in this way from the body, then it would seem capable of existing in the absence of the body. Survival of bodily disintegration is thereby made possible and probable; but it is survival without any bodily frame. Those who find this prospect intolerable (intellectually or practically) will want to reject the dualist theory that gave rise to it. Those who find the possibility of disembodied survival to their taste (say on religious grounds) are invited to consider what they would say about the mind of a pig or a rat: for the considerations that made dualism tempting in the human case would appear to apply equally in these cases – but are we to countenance the idea of the minds of such creatures persisting in disembodied form when they meet their end?

Dualism also has awkward questions to answer in regard to evolution. We are accustomed to the idea (to be discussed further below) that mind somehow developed from matter as matter became organised under the pressure of natural selection; but this idea is surely in conflict with dualism, since the immaterial substance cannot reasonably be supposed to have developed from matter. Are we then to envisage a parallel evolution of immaterial substances somehow harmonised with the evolution of physical organisms? Or should we think that only physical bodies evolve and minds have always existed in their present form, becoming coupled with animal bodies at some time in evolutionary history? In reflecting upon evolution we seem compelled to suppose that mind *somehow* came from matter, but this is something a dualist cannot reasonably accept – and so he finds himself embarrassed by the foregoing questions. Closely connected conceptually with this problem of explaining the sense in which mind 'comes from' matter on a dualist view, there is the notorious difficulty of accounting for causal interaction between mental and physical events if they are to be located in such diverse substances. We generally conceive of causal interaction as proceeding via some sort of mechanism, in such a way that the interacting things engage with each other in some intelligible nexus. But this sort of intelligible connection is precisely what is lacking on the dualist account of mind–body interaction, since the very point of that account is to insist upon the radical difference of nature between mental and physical phenomena. Try to imagine what sort of mechanism might enable material and immaterial substance to come causally together: in so far as you have any conception of the nature of immaterial substance, this must seem a hard task – certainly we cannot legitimately appeal to the sorts of causality mediated by the physical forces studied in the sciences of matter.

The objections to dualism we have rehearsed have not always been found decisive, and there are ways – more or less *ad hoc* – of clinging to the doctrine in the face of them. But dualism is evidently an extravagant and metaphysically repellent theory – a theory we would do better to improve upon if we could. Let us then try to find some more palatable alternative to it and to type-monism.

The position we have reached is this: both monism and dualism have been judged unsustainable, but these may seem to exhaust the field, so the mind–body problem looks insoluble or at least unsolved. Fortunately, however, this pessimistic conclusion need not yet be acceded to; there is a subtler theory to be considered before we despair of finding a satisfactory resolution of our problem. We take a step in the right direction by insisting upon a sharp distinction between the traditional metaphysical categories of substance and attribute – or better, between object and property. The nature of this distinction is the subject of considerable dispute, but the distinction itself is fundamental and very important. The importance of the distinction in the present context is this: from the distinctness of two (sets of) attributes or properties we *cannot* infer the distinctness of the substance or objects which possess those attributes or properties. This principle is sufficiently evident as a general truth about the notions of object and property – consider the obvious fact that one and the same man may have the distinct attributes of being a philosopher and a tennis-player – but it opens up a more interesting possibility in respect of the mind–body relation. Suppose we view mental states as attributes of their subject and physical states as attributes of the body: then from the distinctness of these attributes we cannot, as the above principle proscribes, infer the distinctness of the objects possessing those attributes, namely the psychological subject and his body. So we could hold mental properties to be irreducible and *sui generis* without holding that their subject is a substance or object distinct from any physical object, specifically distinct from the body. This is important because it suggests a way of acknowledging the special nature of mental phenomena without locating them in a realm of incorporeal substances – mental properties may be supposed attributes *of* the body without being *physical* attributes of it.

Now it may be objected to this account of the mind–body relation that it is implausible to treat mental phenomena straightforwardly as properties of their subject, since this ignores the fact that there are mental *events* as much entitled to the status of particular or object as the person undergoing them. That is, if mental events are conceded to be themselves objects possessing attributes, then we are still saddled with *entities* – things which *have* rather than *are* properties – that are non-physical in nature. The question then is what we should say about mental events in the light of this objection that their distinctness from the physical amounts to a dualism of objects and not just of properties. This objection, however, plays right into the hands of the theory it is intended to undermine, by drawing attention to a way of rendering the mind more firmly physical than under the theory that took mental phenomena to be entirely attributive – and doing so without giving up the general commitment to preserving the irreducibility of the mental. For the obvious rejoinder to the objection is to claim that mental events are themselves *identical* with physical events in the brain, though their mental properties are nevertheless distinct from any physical properties of those brain events. The picture, then, is this: consider some particular mental event x and suppose it to be an event of feeling pain (that is, it has the property of being a pain); on the present suggestion this event x is identical with some brain event y which has the property, let us say, of being a C-fibre stimulation – but these two *properties* are not the same. Consider, as an analogy, a single event which is both an assassination of a king and the cause of a revolution – one event exemplifying two properties. We are now in a position to formulate the following thesis: every mental event is identical with some physical event, though the properties in virtue of which an event is mental are not themselves physical properties. Compare: every coloured object is identical with some object having a specific mass, but colour attributes are not mass attributes. This thesis, sometimes referred to as a *token*-identity theory in contrast to the much stronger *type*-identity theory discussed above, is plainly logically consistent; it is also extremely attractive, in that it offers hope of reconciling the two sets of truths about the mental which generate the mind–body problem. It does this by exploiting the distinction between objects and properties: mental phenomena are enmeshed in the physical world in virtue of the identity of mental objects (events) with physical objects (events), but they are not reducible to facts about the physical world because mental properties are not physical properties. Let us call this combination of views *non-reductive monism*.

Given the difficulties encountered by the two extreme doctrines between which non-reductive monism tries to interpose itself, we might be excused for receiving the theory with some enthusiasm: but are there any positive arguments in its favour? One line of thought (there are others) suggestive of non-reductive monism goes as follows. Surveying the world of particular things – daisies, spiders, rocks, books, rain-storms, explosions etc. – we can distinguish two different sorts of attribute under which these particulars fall: some attributes relate to how these particulars *appear* to us, others relate to what we think of as the objective intrinsic nature of particulars. Thus we can describe a particular explosion as loud, and we can describe it in terms of the atomic processes of which it consists: the former description is uninformed by scientific knowledge, the latter depends upon the existence of a properly scientific theory of the event in question. And so it is with particulars at large. But now consider mental particulars and ask yourself whether we can make this sort of distinction in regard to them. Here it seems that the attributes they possess all belong to the non-scientific side, or at least all those attributes which constitute the essential nature of mental particulars: we know of their presence by unaided observation independently of any scientific theory. But particulars in general do not exhibit such one-sidedness: should we then take mental particulars to be exceptions to this general rule? Well, this seems dubious because they do satisfy certain properties which seem to call for the kind of scientifically specified nature mental attributes seem not to supply: they are spatio-temporal entities, possessed of causal powers, and are in some way objectively there in the world. In order to possess these properties, mental particulars, like particulars at large, seem to need some sort of objective reality beyond their appearance to us – the sort of reality that is given by a properly scientific characterisation. If this requirement of mental particulars is plausible, then they must have attributes beyond those we recognise in common-sense mental ascriptions; and it seems that, for want of other possibilities, physical attributes are the kind to fulfil the requirement. This very general and abstract line of thought can be broken down into a number of specific considerations favouring (if not proving) the identification of mental with physical particulars. Of particulars in general it is reasonable to require that they be objective and public, that they be subject to natural laws, and that they have a nature exceeding what common sense recognises. Unless we are to make mental particulars an exception, we need to find a way of according these ubiquitous characteristics to them. But they do not have these characteristics as they are described in ordinary mental vocabulary – or not straightforwardly. Physical descriptions do, however, straightforwardly have these characteristics: describe a particular by ascribing a physical attribute to it, and you describe a particular with the sort of attribute to be objective, law-governed, and possessed of an intrinsic scientific nature. So if we wish mental particulars to have these characteristics, we must acknowledge that they possess the sort of attribute which confers them, that is, physical attributes. We are thus naturally driven to identify mental events with physical events in the brain. Of course this line of thought is not a watertight demonstration of token-identity – it can be questioned at a number of points – but it does provide some considerations giving us positive reason to accept a thesis whose consistency and theoretical motivation we have already noted. What the line of thought relies upon is the point we have stressed throughout, namely that mental phenomena must be seen as in some way bound up in the physical world; there must be *some* sense in which mental events are not different in kind from physical events.

Non-reductive monism, as we have so far stated it, is a rather weak doctrine, because it says nothing about how mental and physical properties are to be related once they have been distinguished: for all we have said, they might be as unrelated as the colour of an object and its mass. Thus token-identity on its own is compatible with the following possibility: that two creatures could have precisely the same physical properties, down to the microstructure of their brains, and yet have *no* mental properties in common – as objects could have the same mass and differ as much as you like in respect of colour. Indeed, token-identity by itself does not even ensure that a creature just like you physically has *any* mental attributes. This degree of independence of the mental with respect to the physical is not acceptable: we want to say that, if two creatures differ mentally, then they differ physically, and that if a creature changes mentally it changes physically. To deny such determination would remove the mental from the physical in an intolerable way. Why do we wish to hold to such determination, though? One way of articulating the force of this dependence thesis is to consider the views we pre-theoretically hold about the relation between mental states and behavioural dispositions on the one hand, and brain states and behavioural dispositions on the other. In the case of many mental states (though perhaps not all) it appears evident that a difference of mental state (uncompensated for by other mental differences) implies a difference of behavioural dispositions; and it also seems undeniable that a difference between the dispositions of two animal bodies depends, other things being equal, upon a difference in their brain states. Suppose then that two creatures had totally different mental attributes, though their brain states were exactly the same. That would imply that their dispositions to behaviour were correspondingly different, even though their brain states differed not at all. But this would be to deny that the brain states of human and animal bodies were responsible for how those bodies are apt to behave. Therefore we must reject the original supposition that mental properties are independent of physical properties. The thesis that the mental is so determined by the physical is sometimes called the *supervenience* thesis: it holds that mental properties cannot vary while physical properties are kept constant. For example, the chemical seems supervenient in this sense on the physical, and the biological on the chemical; and if what we have just said is right, the mental is similarly supervenient on the physical (or neurophysiological).

At this point a worry is likely to assail us: if we conjoin supervenience with token-identity, don't we cancel out the claim of attribute irreducibility? For we seem now to be claiming that, after all, mental properties do have a physical nature – precisely what we have striven to avoid. This worry is not baseless, but we must guard against a mistaken statement of it. The mistaken idea is that the supervenience thesis automatically implies the identity of mental with physical properties. This is a mistake because the dependence claimed by supervenience only goes one way: it says that sameness of physical attributes implies sameness of mental attributes – it does not say that sameness of mental attributes requires sameness of physical attributes. And both directions of dependence would be necessary before attribute *identity* became a feasible proposition. Moreover, supervenience does not, for the same reason, immediately imply that mental attributes have a physical nature: this would be the case only if (what supervenience does not assert) a given mental property could be possessed by a creature only on condition that its brain instantiated the same physical states as other creatures possessing that mental property. Compare clocks: the attribute of being a clock does not have a physical nature or essence, as we can appreciate by considering the many physically different kinds of clock, but it is still true that if two objects are physically indiscernible and one of them is a clock, then so is the other.

But there is a more profound worry to consider; and this springs from the compelling thought that if one sort of fact supervenes on another sort of fact, then it ought to be possible to *explain* how this determination is brought about. That is, it seems reasonable to expect that we be able to say what it is in virtue of which physical properties determine mental properties. The danger here is that we shall find non-reductive monism impaled on the following dilemma: either supervenience is declared to be inexplicable and thus a mystery we are forced to live with; or else it *is* explicable, in which case it would seem that we are awarding a physical nature to mental attributes, since we will be saying what – physically – makes it the case that mental attributes are instantiated in certain complexes of matter. The properties of the brain that are responsible for mentality, if we suppose, following the second alternative, that any are, may relate to the small constituents of brain matter or to more global properties of the brain; the details would, presumably, be discoverable by the sciences of the brain. Essentially the same question arises in regard to the evolution of consciousness, and is sometimes referred to as the problem of *emergence*: if we think, as seems inescapable, that at some stage in evolutionary history matter reached a level of organisation of a kind sufficient for consciousness to come on the scene, then we can ask what it was about matter and its organisation that brought about this momentous innovation. Either we regard this as a mystery, as something we cannot make intelligible, or we suppose there to be an explanation; but it seems that for there to be an explanation of the emergence of consciousness from matter, consciousness must have a physical nature – which we said was very hard to accept. The case appears different with the phenomenon of *life*: this property is also supervenient on the physical – if two things are alike physically, then both are living if one is – but here we do not encounter the same discomfort in acknowledging this fact. There seems no conceptual difficulty in the idea that the attribute of life might result from certain configurations of matter, as we might predict from our earlier observations (in Chapter 1) about borderline cases of life. It is also worth noting that the problem of emergence would not be solved by reverting to dualism; for there would still be the question how consciousness results from configurations of an immaterial substance, given that the consciousness-determining properties are not themselves conscious in nature. What then can be done to alleviate this problem, and will its alleviation leave non-reductive monism intact?

We shall consider two sorts of response to the problem. The first sort of response suggests that we have gone wrong in assuming that matter determines mind in virtue of material properties: what we should say is that matter itself is not purely material in nature, but rather harbours mental properties even *before* it gets organised to form a creature's brain. This view is sometimes called *panpsychism*, because it holds that traces of the mental are to be found in all matter. The view is to be distinguished from *idealism*, which is the doctrine that everything is purely mental; panpsychism claims only that every material thing, even the ultimate constituents of matter, has mental properties in addition to physical ones. The relevance of panpsychism to our present problem is this: in holding that all matter has mental attributes it enables us to say that the mind of an animal results from the combination of the *mental* properties of the matter of the brain, not from its material properties. That is, it locates the origin of mind in properties of matter of the same metaphysical kind as the mental properties for which matter provides the basis, and so avoids the problem of explaining how something of one kind can supervene upon something of a totally different kind. We might compare the principle appealed to by the panpsychist with that involved in the explanation of the rigidity of a building in terms of the rigidity of its constituent *parts* and the way they are put together. As we might anticipate, however there are some very telling objections to panpsychism, as follows.

First, panpsychism is metaphysically and scientifically outrageous. We are being invited to believe that bits of rock and elementary particles enjoy an inner conscious life, on the strength of an a priori argument about how complexes of matter like animals can have minds. But why did we not acknowledge this fact before we came upon the problem of supervenience? Because, simply, mere matter gives no signs of having mental properties, either behavioural or physiological; so there would be no saying *what* mental states these bits of matter possessed. Are we to suppose that rocks actually have thoughts and feelings which they happen to be unable to communicate? Also, do the mental properties of the constituents of matter have any causal powers? Presumably they must if they are to give rise to mental states that do; but how is it, then, that particle physicists have not had to reckon with such causal powers in developing their theories of matter? If the mental properties of electrons bear upon how they will behave, then predictions about them will not be derivable from their physical properties alone: but we know this not to be the case – so the mental properties would have to be declared causally inefficacious. Clearly these accusations of absurdity could be multiplied.

But second, the panpsychist explanation of supervenience only pushes the problem back a stage, or else it undermines its own motivation. For we must now ask whether the mental properties of particles of matter are supervenient on their physical properties. If they are supervenient, then we are back where we started, since we need an explanation of *this* supervenience – only now we cannot appeal to a deeper level of proto-mentality. But if they are not so supervenient, then it becomes unclear why supervenience is obligatory at the macro level – and without such supervenience there would be nothing for panpsychism to explain. It might be replied that it is just a fact that supervenience does not hold at the micro level, and that we take it to hold at the macro level only because we are tacitly crediting matter with proto-psychical properties. But this reply is unconvincing be-cause, first, the intuition of supervenience at the macro level, and the argument for it, did not depend upon tactily attributing mental prop-erties to the constituents of the brain; and, second, we could run the earlier argument for supervenience from considerations about behavi-oural dispositions at the micro level too, now taking behaviour to be the movements and powers of the constituent of matter in question. So either panpsychism compromises its own starting-point or it transfers the problem it is designed to solve to another level.

And third, panpsychism is threatened with the following seemingly insurmountable dilemma: either we suppose pieces of inanimate matter to have fully-fledged consciousness, in particular, sensations and propositional attitudes; or else we suppose such inanimate pieces to be possessed of some sort of proto-consciousness, not yet amounting, in the pieces taken individually, to mentality as we know it. The former alternative is ridiculously extravagant and raises unanswerable questions about why, if this is so, matter ever needed to reach the level of organisation exemplified by the brain before animal consciousness came into being. So it looks as though the panpsychist must intend the latter alternative, in which case the precise character of this proto-consciousness comes into question. And here we quickly see that obscurity on that point is all that prevents the original problem from breaking out again: for if these proto-psychical properties are not already sensations and propositional attitudes, then how can they serve as that from which the properly mental arises? Either elementary particles experience pain or they do not: the former suggestion is absurd; but the latter, in admitting that the proto-psychical falls short of the properly psychical, sacrifices its claim to derive the mind from phenomena of the same kind as mental phenomena. It is only because we do not press the question what *sort* of mental properties inanimate matter has that we suppose panpsychism even in principle capable of solving the problem of emergence.

The second sort of response we shall consider lies at the opposite extreme from panpsychism. Panpsychism took the mind to be radically non-physical and tried to explain its emergence from matter by investing matter with traces of mind; the response we are now to consider purports to offer an account of mind which makes it possible for the merely material to determine its properties. The account is this: the nature of mental attributes is given, not by internal physical states of the organism, but by the *causal role* of those attributes. We are to define mental properties in terms of their typical patterns of cause and effect, including their characteristic stimuli, their interactions with other mental states, and their characteristic effects in behaviour. This doctrine of the nature of mind is sometimes called *functionalism*. Functionalism can be seen as an attempt to explain how mental properties supervene on physical states of the brain: a given brain state will determine a mental property if and only if the brain state has the causal role definitive of the supervening mental property. That is, what makes it the case that a physical state is the kind on which a mental property supervenes is that it has the same causal role as the supervening mental property. This view (if correct) would solve the problem of emergence because we have no difficulty in understanding how a state of the brain could have a specific causal or functional role; and according to functionalism this just *is* what it consists in to have a mental state of a particular kind. But can we accept the functionalist account of the mental?

Functionalism certainly has some signal advantages. It avoids the problem, fatally damaging to type-identity, that different physical states may underlie a given mental state, because different physical mechanisms may have the same functional role; functionalism might, indeed, be said to *explain* this feature of the mental. It also captures the constitutive links with behaviour upon which we earlier remarked, notably in connection with propositional attitudes. It provides the beginnings of an answer to the problem of our knowledge of other minds: since the causal role of a mental state is something objective and publicly detectable, and mental states just consist in their causal role, it seems that the mind must be open to third-person knowledge. And, most importantly for us, it supplies an answer to the problem of emergence. Combining functionalism about mental properties with a token-identity theory of mental particulars would seem to give us a theoretically satisfying conception of the mind. However, attractive as the theory looks, it appears open to a number of more or less severe objections. These are of two sorts: accusations that the theory is, if true, then trivially true; and accusations that the theory is plainly false.

The charge of triviality is this: surely it is true of *any* property that it will be identifiable from a specification of its causal role, if it has one. Any state of an object will have certain characteristic kinds of cause and effect – consider being magnetised or frozen or having C-fibres firing. This is because of the intimate relation between the intrinsic properties of a thing and its dispositional properties: how a thing intrinsically is determines and is determined by the causal dispositions it has. So the question is why a functionalist insists that the nature of a mental state consists in its causal role whereas he does not hold this with respect to physical states and their causal roles. The challenge is to explain why the reasons thought to favour functionalism – chiefly the claim that the causal role of a mental state uniquely identifies it – do not recommend a general functionalist metaphysic: the view that every property, whether mental or physical, can be reduced to a (complex) disposition. Such a metaphysic is dubiously coherent, and obviously relinquishes any ambition of saying what is *distinctive* of the mental. What this point brings out is that it simply doesn't follow from the fact that mental states are *identifiable by* their causal role that they *consist in* their causal role; so some independent argument needs to be adduced to justify drawing this inference in the mental case. And on the face of it the mental is not such as to permit this inference; for we do distinguish, conceptually and linguistically, between intrinsic mental states of a person and the dispositions to which these states give rise. This is shown in the fact that we use ascriptions of mental attributes to *explain* the dispositions to which a person is subject – we say, for example, that a person is disposed to withdraw his hand from the hot water *because* he is in pain as a result of its immersion. But if being in pain were reducible to such dispositions this could not be genuine explanation: it would be like explaining why a substance puts people to sleep by saying it has a dormitive virtue. And this is true quite generally: our practice of using ascriptions of intrinsic properties to things to explain their effects is viable only if those properties are not definable in terms of their effects. Thus the totality of causal disposi-tions of a cup do uniquely fix what it is made of; but we can also explain (some of) those dispositions by citing the composition of the cup – unique identification is thus not the same as property reduction.

The charge of falsity goes further and contests the claim that causal role even identifies a mental state. If this charge can be made to stick, then the functionalist would be embarrassed by the following result: that, in view of the points just made about the reciprocal dependence of *physical* properties and their causal role, mental states are alone in *not* being open to functionalist construal – functionalism would be true of everything *but* the mental! The claim that mental states are not uniquely identified by their causal role is often pressed by considering cases in which we acknowledge that functional description stays con-stant while the phenomenological character of the person's inner states varies. The classic example of this sort of possibility is colour reversal: what one person sees as green another sees as red, though they classify objects and use words in exactly the same way. The simplest and most compelling illustration of this possibility would be two creatures each having monochromatic vision but in distinct colours: their visual fields would look different – they would have different visual experiences – though these experiences have the same causal role. This is presum-ably because their visual experiences carry the same information about the world but do so in what it is tempting to describe as a different phenomenological *medium*. If these cases are really conceivable, as they appear to be, then at least some of the phenomenological aspects of experience cannot be captured in functional terms. Another sort of example intended to make the same point is that of a creature, let us say a rat, which has various sensations but whose functional descrip-tion might be reproduced in an insentient robot: it seems perfectly conceivable that a robot be so designed as precisely to reproduce the propensities of a minded rat – and if so, functional properties would be insufficient to guarantee even the presence of mental properties.

It is worth noting that we cannot readily produce such cases in respect of propositional attitudes, unless we base them upon cases in which experiences are varied. Thus we can say that the creature with red experiences will believe that things are red, since he will exercise the concept *red* in judgements about the perceived world; while the creature who sees things as green will believe objects of perception to be green: different beliefs, same causal role. But it is doubtful that we could preserve functional role by permuting beliefs whose content did not differ in this derivative way. This difference between sensations and propositional attitudes evidently relates to the point that our conception of the latter ties them more closely to behaviour and the third-person perspective; the first-person perspective on sensations is what induces us to regard them as independent of behaviour in the ways exploited by the above counter-examples to functionalism. It is not that such examples are entirely uncontroversial – too much hangs on them for that – but they should give us serious misgivings about accepting the functionalist account of supervenience. Once again the special character of consciousness frustrates attempts to explain its nature in other terms. Functionalism is not the answer to our problems.

Our efforts to arrive at a satisfactory theory of the relation between mind and body have not met with total success. We have, it is true, gone some way towards explaining how the mind can be different in nature from the body yet be intimately connected with it. But we have not explained how a physical organ of the body, namely the brain, could be the basis of consciousness – how a physical object can come to have an 'inner' aspect. One might be tempted to conclude that the mind–body problem, so stated, is insoluble: but it is hard to see how we can really accept this pessimistic conclusion, for surely there *is* something about brains that makes them conscious, whether we can know and understand it or not. We should persist in the hope that some day philosophy (or perhaps science) will find the answer.

3 Acquaintance with things

One of the most important characteristics of mind is the capacity to be aware *of* various things. Indeed, this other-directedness seems to be an *essential* characteristic of mind: to be conscious is to be conscious of this or that item. In the present chapter we shall examine the nature of this relation of acquaintance: that is, what is involved in states or acts of mind which are directed on to things other than themselves. We shall begin by discussing perceptual acquaintance, moving on to other varieties of acquaintance; and we shall want to know whether a uniform account of the different species of acquaintance is possible.

Let us consider a commonplace example of perception – seeing a particular book on the table. In such a case we can distinguish between two aspects of the situation: we can specify which object it is that is seen, and we can specify the way in which it is seen – what it is seen *as*. The former specification involves identifying a particular object in the external world and saying that it stands in a certain relation to the perceiver; the form of the specification is thus '*a* sees *b*' – where 'sees' expresses a dyadic (two-termed) relation. The latter specification addresses itself to the character of the perceiver's experience; it says how things *look* to him. Let us employ the locution 'has an experience as of' in specifying this second aspect of the perceptual situation; then we can say that in the above example the perceiver has an experience as of a book of such and such a character. And let us say that such an 'as of' locution gives the *content* of the perceiver's experience – how the experience represents the world as being. This idea of the content of an experience is to be distinguished from the idea of the *object* of the experience, the external object to which the perceiver is perceptually related. Roughly speaking, the content of the experience is a matter of how things *seem* to you, while the perceptual object is the actual external thing that seems that way. So of any perceptual experience we can always ask two questions: 'What is the object of the experience?' and 'What is the content of the experience?' These questions are clearly quite distinct, though their distinctness can be masked by the ambiguity of the question 'What is this an experience of?' One immediate difference to note, which shows the distinctness of the questions, is that the former question may receive the answer 'nothing' while the latter question can never receive this answer: an experience may lack an object, if it is a case of total hallucination, but it cannot lack a content – having a content is a condition of its very existence. With these elements of the perceptual situation distinguished we can ask the following questions: What is the nature of the dyadic perceptual relation between a person's experience and its object? How is the content of an experience to be conceived? What is the connection between perceptual object and perceptual content?

To make progress on the first two questions we should remind ourselves of some truisms bearing upon the third question. Thus, it should be plain that the content of an experience does not uniquely identify its object: since there are, or could be, many books in the world which equally 'fit' the content of an experience as of a book with such and such features, we cannot think that what constitutes or establishes the relation to a particular perceptual object is just the content of the experience. This failure of determination as between content and object is shown in a second truism, namely that an experience may *mis*represent its object: that is, the content of an experience may be as of an object with features the actual object of perception does not, in point of fact, possess – how things seem is not always how things are. The most vivid cases of this are the various sorts of visual illusion dealt with by the psychologist of perception, for example the Müller–Lyer illusion, in which lines of equal length look unequal. But it is important to note that a misrepresenting experiential content does not automatically prevent the misrepresented object from being the object perceived: you do not cease to see a thing just because your experience credits it with properties it does not objectively have. From these truisms we can derive the thesis that content and object are, in a certain sense, mutually independent: we cannot deduce the content of an experience from knowledge of its object (though we may be able to guess at it); and we cannot deduce the identity of the object of a perceptual experience from knowledge of its content (though again we can often make informed guesses). In short, the conditions which constitute, respectively, the content and the object of a perceptual experience are logically independent. As a corollary, experiences could have the same content but different objects, or the same object but different contents. No analysis of perceptual acquaintance could be correct, therefore, which failed to respect this two-way independence.

It follows from what we have just established that the content of experience is not to be specified by using terms that refer to the object of experience, on pain of denying that distinct objects can seem precisely the same: so when we are describing the content of an experience we should not make singular reference to the object of the experience in the context following 'as of'. In fact it seems right to uphold a stronger thesis about experiential content: that an accurate description of the phenomenological content of an experience will employ only *general* terms to specify how the experience represents the world. Thus we are to say that a given experience is as of *a* book that is brown, thick and has the words 'The Bible' inscribed on it; we are not to say, when giving the content of the experience, *which* book it is that is seen. It is true that, in so far as we ever describe the content of our experiences in daily life, we do sometimes in so doing refer to particular objects: we may say that we seemed to see *Jones* just now, not that we seemed to see *a* man with black hair, reddish complexion etc. But this way of talking appears to result from allowing associated *beliefs* to enter our descriptions of experience: the true position is that we have experiences whose content is wholly general and we believe that a particular object meets those general conditions; so we naturally but misleadingly mention that object in saying how things seem to us. This is abetted by the ambiguity of 'seems': there is the strictly phenomenological use of the word, which is the use we are here interested in, and there is the use which heralds the expression of a tentative belief. The intuition to cling to is that things would seem the same to you even if you did not form the belief that the object you were perceiving was Jones – this belief is something superimposed upon the experience itself. This thesis, that experience is inherently and essentially general in its mode of representation, is sometimes put by saying that experience is purely 'qualitative'; but in view of the danger of confusion with another way in which this word is used to characterise experience, namely to register its subjectivity, it is better to express the present point by saying that the content of experience is to be specified in terms of general concepts alone. This generality thesis explains why it is that the content of an experience does not determine its object, in conjunction with the observation that the general concepts used to specify experiential content do not (typically) uniquely identify the perceptual object; indeed it is hard to see how this latter truism could hold unless the generality thesis were correct. On the other hand, it seems that to specify the object of experience we do need to employ genuine reference to particular objects: thus we standardly pick out perceptual objects by using proper names like 'Jones' or demonstratives like 'that cat' – as in 'Smith sees Jones' or 'Brown sees that cat.'

The generality thesis, as we have formulated it so far, does not quite go far enough in restricting the sort of vocabulary that may be used in specifying phenomenological content. The content of experience is ascribed by using general concepts applicable to things in the world; but some, indeed many, general concepts apply to things in the world in virtue of properties not fully manifest to the senses, for example the concepts of *tiger* or *water*. Such concepts hold of things in virtue of their 'inner constitution' – being H_2O or having a certain genetic structure. This means that it is possible for things to have the same *appearance* as tigers and water yet not fall under the concepts *tiger* and *water*; so there would be no phenomenological difference between experiences whose content was specified using one of those concepts rather than the concepts appropriate to the things that merely have the same appearance as tigers and water. We should therefore restrict the concepts invoked to characterise content to those that relate to the appearances of things – concepts of colour, superficial texture, shape etc. In this way we limit our ascriptions of content to how things *seem* to the perceiver.

The content of experience comprises the mode of perceptual presentation of the object to the perceiver; it contains how the world is represented in experience, and so the manner in which the mind apprehends the objects of perceptual acquaintance. Our earlier conclusions can now be summarised in the thesis that perceptual modes of presentation neither contain nor determine which object is thereby presented – the singularity of the perceptual object is otherwise fixed.

Having clarified the structure of acts of perceptual acquaintance we can now address the following three questions: (*a*) What is the nature of the dyadic relation of perceiving an object? (*b*) What determines the psychological significance of an act of perceptual acquaintance? (*c*) How seriously should we take talk of experiences *representing* objects?

We already know that the answer to question (*a*) cannot be that the object of perception is the object which *fits* the content of the experience, since an object may fit the general conditions comprised in the perceptual mode of presentation and yet not be perceived, and the object perceived may fail to fit the content of the experience. The missing ingredient seems to be a *causal* relation between the object and the experience: it is a necessary condition of perceiving an object that the experience be causally dependent on the object. Of course we know that, as a matter of empirical fact, our perceptual experiences do depend upon a causal connection with the object perceived; but it also seems evident enough that it is part of the *concept* of perception that the dyadic perceptual relation is a species of causal relation. The concept of memory is comparable in this respect: it is not conceptually possible to remember an earlier event unless your memory of it is the end result of a causal chain originating in the event in question. It is thus very plausible to construe the relation of perception as a special case of the causal relation. To say this is not to claim that we can fully *analyse* perception causally – in particular, it is not to say that *sufficient* conditions for perception can be given in causal terms. In fact there seems to be a very general and intractable difficulty in the way of achieving such an analysis, which emerges when we consider certain kinds of non-standard causal connections that may obtain between objects and experiences. Suppose you have an experience as of an eye of such and such a character which you are caused to have because of a malfunction in your own eye: then the fact that the experience was caused by something precisely matching it, that is, the experience as of an eye was caused by the eye, does not guarantee that you *see* your eye. What we have in this case is a kind of *accidental* matching of content and object mediated by a causal chain. It is probably impossible to specify in a non-circular manner what sorts of causal chain make for genuine perception; but for our purposes it is not necessary to claim that a full causal analysis is possible – it is enough to note that perception necessarily involves a causal relation with the object, though of a kind not isolable without using the notion of perception itself.

This causal picture of the perception relation is confirmed by an important feature of our concept of perception, namely that we distinguish between mediate and immediate perceptual objects. We allow, that is, that one object may be perceived *by* perceiving another, as when you see a cat by seeing its head. In general we allow that objects may be seen in virtue of their parts – indeed surfaces of their parts – being seen, rather as we allow that an object may be touched by touching its parts or their surfaces. If we did not operate the concept of perception in this way we would, in a sense, perceive much less than we do – we would see only parts or surfaces of things. Conceiving perception as causal provides some sort of explanation for this, because we similarly operate with a distinction between mediate and immediate causation: a mediate cause of an event is one which causes it in virtue of some other cause, as when we say a car caused a death by way of its bumper. We thus allow the causal relation to be transmitted through the part–whole relation. So if we construe the perception relation as a kind of causal relation, we can regard mediate and immediate perceptual objects as corresponding to mediate and immediate causes; and indeed it is plausible that we make judgements as to what is mediately perceived on the basis of principles linking causation with part–whole relations.

A person's perception of the world clearly plays a role in his psychology: perception gives rise to beliefs which interact with other elements of the mind to lead to intelligent action. We may refer to this psychological role as the *significance* of an act of perceptual acquaintance for the perceiver. Upon what does this significance depend? It depends, evidently, upon how the world is represented as being, since this is what functions as the basis of belief and thence action. The relational aspect of perception, in contrast, has no such psychological signifi-cance, since it consists in facts which are, in an obvious sense, outside the mind. Thus what affects behaviour in perceptual situations is just how things seem to you. This can be appreciated by considering cases of hallucination: if hallucinatory experiences are produced in you, without your knowing them to be such, which exactly match veridical experiences in their content, then you will behave just as you would were you in the perceptual relation to objects. So when we explain why someone reached for a cup of coffee by saying that he *saw* the cup this can be philosophically misleading in two ways: first, in that it might suggest that we need not consider *how* he saw the cup, whether he saw it *as* a cup; and second, it might suggest that, even when the relevance of the content of the experience is made clear, the relational aspect is itself doing explanatory work in determining psychological signifi-cance. In fact such explanatory statements appear tantamount to 'He *seemed* to see a cup, and there was a cup where he seemed to see it.' The case is similar with belief and knowledge: how your beliefs dispose you to act is independent of whether they rank as knowledge; so explaining someone's action of crossing the road by saying that he *knows* that the bank is open is a potentially misleading way of saying that he did it because he *believes* that the bank is open. In both cases whether the world complies with how you represent it is strictly irrelevant to the psychological significance of the representation. But if it is the content of experience that determines psychological significance and hence explanatory force, then general concepts suffice to capture all that is relevant in a person's experience to his dispositions to form beliefs and act: mention of particular objects is not needed to characterise the psychological role of an act of perceptual acquaintance.

We have spoken of perceptual 'representation': how conceptually close is this to other kinds of representation – is it, in particular, anything like pictorial representation? It is curiously tempting to conceive of perceptual experiences as like little pictures in the mind; but this conception is really very problematic. One obvious difference between experiences and pictures is that we do not become acquainted with the objects of perception by *looking at* experiences; indeed if that were our relation to experiences we should not be properly acquainted with external objects at all (we return to this issue). So if experiences were anything like pictures they must connect with our cognitive apparatus quite differently from the way real pictures do. Pictures connect with the mind in virtue of their intrinsic characteristics: a painting is executed in a particular medium, with particular colours, with certain spatial arrangements of paint – and in looking at the painting we are aware of those intrinsic characteristics and hence of what they represent. We can thus offer two sorts of description of a painting: intrinsic descriptions, and representational descriptions – for example, that the painting is in oils and that it is of a horse, respectively. Now if experiences were pictorial we should expect such a distinction to apply to them also. But on the face of it intrinsic descriptions of experience are hard to come by; descriptions of experience seem to be wholly of the representational sort – they tell us what the experience is as of rather than what it is like intrinsically. Experiences seem, paradoxically, like pictures in no medium – that is, not really pictures at all. However, closer inspection suggests that experiences do have *some* intrinsic properties: we speak of an experience as occurring at a certain time and lasting a certain stretch of time, as distinct from the time of that which is experientially represented; we locate the experience in space, roughly where the perceiver is; we may speak of *parts* of the visual field, as when we say that we have a blind spot which produces a gap in the visual field; and it seems legitimate to say that one object takes up literally *more* of our visual field than another, even though it does not look bigger. But it is harder to point to some feature of experience that might qualify as a *medium* of mental representation – the 'stuff' of experience, so to speak. And without such a medium, talk of representation in the perceptual and pictorial cases cannot be regarded as univocal. If any medium of mental representation is to be found, it would appear that we need to look beyond what is presented to us in having experience to other features experiences might possess. A radical suggestion, on these lines, is that we have been looking in the wrong place for the medium and so, not surprisingly, have failed to find it: we should have looked to the *material* basis of experience in the brain. On this suggestion, then, the medium of experiential representation is the brain matter and its physical properties: neurophysiological configurations are to experiential content what arrangements of paint are to pictorial content. The difference, it may be suggested, is that we are aware, perceptually, of the latter medium but not of the former; and this is precisely because we look at paintings and only *have* experiences. This suggestion at least has the advantage of justifying literal talk of representation in application to perceptual experience; but it is rather too ingenious to be instantly appealing. Let it suffice to say, inconclusively, that a strict analogy with pictorial representation is sustainable only under some such view.

It should be noted that aspects of representational content are quite distinct from intrinsic properties in the sense just discussed. The question then arises as to whether intrinsic properties of experience play a causal role in the mind in addition to the role played by representational properties. If they do, then it would surely be a very different sort of role from that played by representational content, since it will not relate to how the world is apprehended as being; it will not consist in having a certain *significance*. The answer seems to be that intrinsic properties do have *some* role, but the matter is delicate and controversial. Thus consider what happens to your visual field if you close one eye: there is a clear sense in which the visual field gets smaller, and this shrinkage affects the psychological role of the visual field in an obvious way. It is very tempting to describe this as a change in the intrinsic properties of experience, with a certain psychological upshot. But someone may insist that this misdescribes the phenomenon: what we should say is simply that less of the world is represented after one eye is closed. The difficulty of deciding between these two descriptions of what is going on in this case brings out some of the conceptual perplexities surrounding the nature of experience. Let us be content to have formulated some of the questions that need to be asked here.

We have spoken of the mind as populated by experiences in the having of which the perceiver is brought into acquaintance with external objects. This sort of account of perceptual acquaintance has often been thought to introduce a certain indirection into our acquaintance with the external world: the account has been supposed to commit us to the idea that the immediate objects of acquaintance are really the experiences themselves and not the external objects we commonly take them to be experiences of – or worse that the existence of experiences puts up an impenetrable wall between the perceiving subject and the world outside him. We may thus be presented with the following dilemma: either we accept this consequence, like it or not, or we give up the idea of inner representing experiences altogether. It is worth taking some time to show that this dilemma is spurious, in view of its perennial allure.

The thesis against which the dilemma is directed is that we get to be acquainted with external objects by means of, or in virtue of, the having of experiences with content, which experiences are caused by those objects; the worry is that the experiences will, on this picture, come between us and the world. A quick way to see that this worry is groundless is to compare perceiving an object with referring to an object. When we use a word to refer to something we make that thing the object of a representational act; and we do so by uttering a certain sound or inscribing a certain mark. Reference thus involves three items: speaker, word, object. Uttering the word is the means whereby we refer to the object; we mention an object *by* using a word. None of these platitudes is at all problematic: no one supposes that the use of words to refer to objects introduces any indirection into the act of reference, that the immediate object of reference is the word itself, or that we do not really refer to objects at all but only to words. Such suppositions would rest upon a confusion between use and mention, between sign and object. There are, similarly, three items involved in perception: perceiver, experience, object. The having of the experience is analogous to the uttering of a word: in virtue of having the experience an external object comes to be an object of perceptual acquaintance. To suppose that the involvement of an inner experience produces perceptual indirection, or enclosure in a world of merely mental objects of acquaintance, is the analogue of a use–mention confusion. This is not to say that it is false that we are acquainted with our own experiences – we are, on the contrary, acquainted with them in acts of introspection – but it does not follow that we are not also and primarily acquainted with external objects. We should be careful not to confuse two distinct acts of the mind: acquaintance with objects by dint of having perceptual experiences, and acquaintance with experiences by virtue of introspective acts. We may, likewise, on occasion refer to our own words, but this does not mean that we never refer to objects. Even if every act of perceptual acquaintance were also and simultaneously an act of introspective acquaintance with the perceptual experience, we need only to distinguish the acts to avoid the conclusion that experiences are the genuine objects of perceptual awareness.

Other considerations have led philosophers to this erroneous conclusion, but when these are made explicit they are easily seen to be devoid of force; we shall briefly mention three such considerations just to set them aside. One fallacious line of reasoning is this: suppose we define the immediate object of perceptual acquaintance to be that item which is perceived but not in virtue of perceiving some other item. Then we will be led to envisage a series of items standing in a relation of perceptual derivativeness – going perhaps from whole objects to their parts and thence to surfaces of their parts. But it may be supposed that we can go a step further: since we perceive objects in virtue of having experiences, we also perceive their surfaces in virtue of having experiences – *ergo* experiences themselves must be the immediate objects of perception. The fallacy here is to move from 'We perceive things in virtue of having experiences' to 'We perceive things in virtue of *perceiving* experiences'; and we cannot *argue* to the latter thesis on the basis of the above definition of the immediate object of perception, since this patently begs the question. Gross as this fallacy is, reasoning close to it has been surprisingly influential.

A second bad line of argument trades upon an idea of causal proximity to push the proper objects of acquaintance into the mind: it is supposed that since experiences are causally 'nearer' to the subject than external objects are, in the sense that they are later items on the causal chain reaching from the object to the perceiving subject, we should say that it is they which are *immediately* apprehended. But it is simply false that each item on such a causal chain is a perceptual object, and events in the optic nerve are obviously not better candidates for being perceived than the tables and chairs that initiate the causal chains in which they occur. Besides, words are (generally) spatially and causally more proximate to us than the objects they refer to; but it would be ludicrous to conclude that words are the immediate objects of reference. This line of thought simply confuses the logic of one sort of relation with the logic of another.

A third consideration that has weighed heavily with some is a certain equivocation in the notion of acquaintance – a tendency to build two quite distinct concepts into its definition. On the one hand, there is the idea of that of which we are underivatively aware – things directly present to the mind without any process of reasoning. On the other hand, there is the idea of objects whose nature and existence is incorrigibly known to the subject – things about which he cannot have false beliefs. If we suppose, illicitly, that the former idea entails the latter, then we shall find ourselves withholding the former title from objects which fail to qualify for the latter: in particular, external objects, since they are not infallibly known, will be declared not directly present to awareness. The cure for this temptation to deny that we are acquainted with external objects is simply to distinguish the two ideas; and there is no contradiction in the notion of an object of direct perceptual awareness with respect to which our beliefs are fallible. We can therefore retain the common-sense belief that we unproblematically *see* tables and chairs – that we are capable of direct mental contact with things outside us.

We now have an account of the structure of perceptual acquaintance; our next question is whether, and if so how, this account may be carried over to the representative content of propositional attitudes. For simplicity let us consider beliefs formed as a result of perceptual experience, for example the belief that this cup is cracked or that Jones has red hair. When we consider the character of the *aboutness* of these beliefs – their being beliefs about this cup or about Jones – it seems entirely natural to characterise this relation by using materials drawn from our account of perception. Thus suppose you see the cracked cup under a particular mode of presentation; then your subsequent thoughts about the cup will presumably involve some sort of memory trace of this mode of presentation – the concepts under which you bring the cup in your thoughts about it will match the concepts which specify the content of your past experience. If a belief is thus derived from perceptual acquaintance, then the way in which its subject-matter is later *con*ceived will follow the way in which it was earlier *per*ceived. From this it appears to follow that to specify the conceptual mode of presentation involved in beliefs of this basic kind we should employ only general concepts. And now if we were to identify the propositional content of a belief with the combination of concepts under which the objects of belief are conceived, we would then reach the conclusion that the content of beliefs is itself entirely general. This is a conclusion many philosophers have wanted to accept, though they have not explicitly derived this generality thesis in the way we just have. But the generality thesis in respect of thought content appears radically controverted by our actual practice in ascribing thoughts; for we do ascribe singular thoughts – thoughts whose specification involves mention of particular objects. We can respond to this collision of theory and practice in one of three ways: we can decide that we must have been wrong about experiential content; we can refrain from identifying the propositional content of perceptual beliefs with experiential content or memory traces thereof; or we can claim that thought content is latently or ultimately purely general in character and recommend the elimination of singular ascriptions. The approach we shall take here is the second of these. This view enables us to retain our account of perceptual modes of presentation, accept nevertheless that there are genuinely singular thoughts, and also allow that conceptual modes of presentation derive from perceptual ones. The key to maintaining all these together is to deny that the conceptual content of a belief exhausts its total content. Roughly speaking, we regard the content of a perceptual belief as comprising *both* the associated experiential content, which is purely general, *and* the perceptual object, which is (of course) perfectly singular. Thus if we want to know which singular proposition someone believes we need to be told both which concepts are involved in the mode of presentation and which objects the belief is about. Knowledge of the concepts alone will not suffice, since they will typically not uniquely identify the object, and may indeed misrepresent it if the content of the original experience was inaccurate. Thus the belief about the cup may derive from an experience in which the cup is represented under concepts which apply to many cups in the world, and perhaps under concepts that fail to apply to that cup – it may seem, for example, to be white when in fact it is blue. A good way to appreciate how perceptual content may fail to determine belief content is to imagine cases in which numerically distinct objects look exactly the same, either to two people or to one person on two occasions: the corresponding beliefs will be about different objects, but the way those objects are conceived will be the same, given that manner of conception derives wholly from manner of perception. These considerations also make it natural to regard the relational element of the belief as causal in character, perhaps supplemented with an extra segment taking in the memory trace. So the content of a belief, this being identified with the proposition believed, will combine, in effect, the content of a perceptual experience and the object of that experience. Before we try to explain *why* our notion of belief content behaves in this way, let us note a consequence of this conception of belief.

The consequence to note is that if a perceptual experience lacks an object, because it is hallucinatory, then no belief based upon that experience can have the complete content it would have were the experience veridical: that is, the singular belief which would have resulted had an object been perceived does not in fact result. The state which results does involve a mode of presentation, identical to that which would have accompanied the singular belief had it been formed; but since the state is about no particular object, it does not have the propositional content it purports to have – which implies, perhaps surprisingly, that we can be wrong about the content of our thoughts.

We can see from examples that belief content combines both general modes of presentation and particular objects, but can we offer any explanation of why belief content has these two ingredients? It does not seem promising to seek the rationale of both ingredients in the psychological significance of a belief, since this will be exhausted by the general mode of presentation inherited from the content of the prompting perceptual experience. This consideration does, however, place one component of belief content in its proper place: the general mode of presentation of the object of belief is what is needed to determine the psychological role of the belief. So it seems that the singular component of content will have to be sought elsewhere than in psychological significance. The natural answer to the question as to why belief content absorbs the perceptual object is this: beliefs are relations to propositions, and propositions are bearers of truth and falsity; but truth and falsity turn on the condition of objects in the world; so to get the truth conditions of a belief right we have to reckon with objects. Thus in a case of beliefs concerning different objects whose mode of presentation is the same we need to include the objects themselves in the respective propositions or else we shall have nothing with which to distinguish the truth conditions. To put it differently, we acknowledge singular belief contents because truth conditions concern external objects, and these are not determined by the believer's modes of conception. Thus it is that two concerns we have with beliefs come together in our conception of their content: we are concerned with beliefs as explanatory states of the person, and this concern calls upon the general modes of conceiving objects derived in the most basic case from perception; and we are concerned with them as propositional attitudes which we can assess for truth and falsity, and this concern calls for acknowledgement of a relational aspect to content. We can ask two sorts of question about someone's beliefs: how they dispose him to act, and whether they are true. In view of the great difference between these two questions it is perhaps not surprising that belief content should combine two distinct ingredients. The two ingredients are as logically independent as the content of perception and its object, as we might expect from the intimate connection between beliefs about the external world and the perceptions on which they are based.

So far we have confined our discussion of the nature of acquaintance to the perception of external things and thoughts based thereon; we must now turn our attention to other species of acquaintance with other sorts of object. The nature of these other species is a more difficult matter, but it will help if we keep the perception case in mind as a model and ask whether other types of acquaintance have a similar structure and mechanism. The question to answer, then, is whether we can give a uniform account of acquaintance in general. A full discussion of this would require us to treat of such objects of awareness or thought as numbers, properties, instants or stretches of time, points or regions of space – entities that cannot be said to be in any straightforward way perceptible. But any adequate account of these types of acquaintance must wait upon a metaphysical account of the nature of the *objects* of such acquaintance; we cannot say what it is to be acquainted with these until we know what kinds of item they are – in particular, until we know whether they can be *causes* of mental acts of acquaintance. These issues, however, go beyond our purview: but there are two sorts of acquaintance which directly engage with some of the most central questions in the philosophy of mind – namely, acquaintance with one's own mental states and acquaintance with one's self – and we must try to shed some light on their nature. We begin with the former, introspective acquaintance.

Suppose you have an experience as of the setting sun, accompanied by the judgement 'The sun looks very red tonight.' Granted that it is really the sun that you are seeing, you are acquainted with the sun and your judgement is about that object of acquaintance. But now suppose you turn your attention, as we say, inward, taking the experience itself as object and judge 'This experience is as of the setting sun.' It seems, then, that you are aware *of* the experience and that the words 'this experience' refer to that of which you are aware: you judge about something mental from the first-person perspective – something that others might judge about from the third-person perspective. Or again, you can take your bodily sensations, such as pain, as objects of introspective acquaintance and make corresponding judgements about those sensations. It seems natural to take this primitive introspective awareness to be parallel to the perception of external things, and the corresponding judgement about the object of that introspective awareness to be parallel to judgements about external things based upon perception of them: in both cases we have a basic dyadic relation of acquaintance upon which is superimposed a propositional attitude whose subject-matter comprises the object of that acquaintance. Can we then analyse the relation of introspective acquaintance as we analysed perceptual acquaintance? Can we break the relation down into an act with a certain 'as of' content specifiable in purely general terms, and a particular object causing this act of introspective acquaintance? If we wished to hold, as many have, that introspection is a modality of perception, then it seems that the answer must be affirmative; but we shall see that there are difficulties in the way of this.

One thing that seems clear is that introspective awareness is not itself a kind of *experience*: you do not have an experience as of your experience as of the sun setting. This is because the act of inner awareness does not have the phenomenology characteristic of a sense modality. The only phenomenology attending such awareness comes from the *object* of the awareness; but if introspection really were a form of sense-perception we should expect it to bring its own distinctive phenomenology to its acts of acquaintance, which could in principle be quite different from that manifested by the object of acquaintance. So we can safely say that introspection does not consist in *experiencing* the contents of one's mind, at least in the usual acceptation of that word. However, it does not seem wrong to credit introspective acts with general content – to say that your awareness was as of *an* experience as of the setting sun. That the content of such mental acts is thus general is shown by the consideration that if you had a numerically distinct experience of the same qualitative character as the given one, then the content of the introspective act would be the same. Thus when you are aware of a particular pain the content of your introspective awareness brings the pain under general concepts, and a distinct particular pain could be brought under the same concepts: we do not say that your awareness is as of *that* pain, but that it is as of a pain of such-and-such a general character. The content of the introspective awareness accordingly does not suffice to determine *which* pain you are aware of; this must be determined by factors extraneous to the introspective content. A judgement about a pain will, though, bring the particular pain itself into the content of the proposition judged, and for the same reason as in the case of perceptual judgements.

So it seems that introspective acquaintance at least has the same sort of *structure* as perceptual acquaintance; but is the relational element of it also analogous to the relation of perception? Since we are allowing causal relations between states of mind in general, there seems no very good reason for denying that some mental states may cause others which constitute an awareness of the causing state: thus your experience causes your introspective act of awareness of it. But to allow this is very far from affirming a strict analogy with the causal account of the perception relation, still less that the claim of causal connection amounts to a complete theory of how the introspective dyadic relation is established. Suspicions are raised by the difficulty of finding anything corresponding to the problem of non-standard causal chains: it is precisely because we cannot raise this as a *problem* for a full causal analysis of the introspective relation that the claim of causal connection begins to look conceptually trivial – it looks too easy. Let us try to imagine a case in which a particular pain causes an act of introspective awareness as of a pain but the awareness is not in fact a case of introspecting that pain. The difficulty here seems to be, to put it shortly, that we cannot make sense of introspective hallucinations: that is, any awareness as of a pain must take a pain as object – but then we will not be able to devise a case in which a pain causes an act of introspective awareness which act is not *of* that pain. The only possibility would be one pain causing an awareness of another pain, but this is impossible to make sense of. Causal connections between acts of mind and its contents cannot fail to be cases of introspection; so introspective acquaintance does not, in this respect, parallel what we find in the case of perception of external objects. The relation of introspection has the look of something primitive and unanalysable – more so than perception. Still, this difference does not require us to give up the thesis that the two species of acquaintance have the same basic structure of general content directed to particular object.

If introspective awareness is problematic, how much more so is *self-*awareness. We shall return to the self in Chapter 6, but some comments must now be ventured regarding acquaintance with the self, though these will, to some extent, presuppose a certain conception of the nature of the self, to be elaborated upon when the time comes. To have self-acquaintance is to be aware of that which is referred to by 'I', as when one makes a judgement of the form 'I am thus-and-so.' As one may be aware of one's visual experience as of the setting sun and make a judgement about that experience, so one may be aware of *oneself* as having an experience as of the setting sun and make a judgement about the self which has that experience – expressed as '*I* am having an experience etc.' Here again it seems that we have to do with a basic dyadic relation, this time between the subject and himself, on the foundation of which a self-ascriptive judgement may be made. The question, then, is whether this act of self-awareness parallels the acts of perception and introspection. But before we attempt to answer this question, we should note some connections between acquaintance with the self and acquaintance with the contents of the mind: for it is very plausible that a creature has the former sort of acquaintance if and only if it has the latter. That is to say, if a creature is aware of its own experiences, then it is aware of them as *its* experiences; and if it is aware of itself, then it must also be introspectively aware of its states of mind. When you are aware of your experience as of the setting sun, you are aware of the experience as *your* experience as of the setting sun; and when you make a self-ascriptive judgement you must in that very act be aware of the contents of your own mind. Self-acquaintance and introspective acquaintance thus seem to be interdependent. It stands otherwise with perceptual acquaintance: this seems to require neither of the other two sorts of acquaintance. Consider unreflective animals, their awareness perpetually glued on to the external world for fear of what will befall them: they are certainly aware of objects in their environment, but have not the luxury of thoughts about their own mental states and selves (if indeed they have selves: we return to this in

Chapter 6). Not for nothing is introspective awareness commonly described as *self*-consciousness: the self is not in fact its proper object, but it is true that there is no introspective awareness of mental states without awareness of their subject.

With respect to whether self-acquaintance mirrors perceptual acquaintance in its structure, three questions are apposite: Do we have *experience* of the self? Does the act of self-awareness have general representational content? Is the self causally responsible for acts of acquaintance with it? There is one conception of the self on which the answer to each question is affirmative: this is the view that the self may be identified with the *body*. For if the self *is* the body, then it must be true that we perceive the self, since we perceive the body; and if self-acquaintance is just a kind of sense perception, then it will have the characteristics of perceptual acquaintance simply by virtue of being a special case of it. We are acquainted with the body by way of vision, touch, smell etc., and by the internal senses of proprioception and kinaesthesia; on the body view of the self these senses are what make us aware of the referent of 'I'. When these senses are turned on the body (as the last two are by definition) we have experiences with a certain general content, and these experiences are caused by states of the body. Plainly, the acceptability of this view of self-acquaintance depends upon the acceptability of the view of the self it is premised on – a view we will later find *un*acceptable; but we can do something now to discredit the view by considering whether self-acquaintance does in fact depend upon bodily acquaintance. Two sorts of possibility, the second more extreme than the first, show that it does not. The first is the case of a person whose experiences as of his body being thus-and-so are wholly hallucinatory: he might be the subject of an experiment in which all input from his senses is occluded and his brain stimulated by the experimenter to produce a phenomenological simulacrum of body perception. It appears evident that this person could still be self-aware and make judgements about himself; but this would not be mediated by acquaintance with his body, since, by hypothesis, he has no such acquaintance. The second case involves imagining that the sensory input is again occluded but no phenomenological simulacrum is produced: there is just a phenomenological blank where before there was a rich phenomenal field. Since this person would still enjoy conscious states not of the kind resulting from perception – headaches, visual images, thoughts etc. – he could still be self-aware; so self-awareness does not depend even on *seeing* perceptions of one's body. These two sorts of case show that awareness of the self is not constituted by awareness of the body.

These considerations also refute a weaker version of the thesis that self-acquaintance is body-acquaintance, a version which does not rely on an *identification* of self with body. This is the idea that there is some relation between self and body such that awareness of the self is transmitted from awareness of the body through that relation. The thought here is that just as the part–whole relation transmits perception of a part of an object to the object of which it is a part, so the self might be related to the body in just such a way: since the body is perceived, the self would then be an object of transferred perception. The trouble with this suggestion is not so much that no such relation exists – for our habit of saying that we see and hear and touch other *persons* and not just their bodies suggests that we do acknowledge the existence of such a relation – the trouble is rather that self-awareness can be present though body-awareness is not, as in the above imaginary cases. If this is right, then acquaintance with the self cannot be explained in terms of transferred perceptual acquaintance with the body.

A second suggestion seeking to explain self-awareness in terms of materials already at our disposal is the thesis that acquaintance with self is just a special case of introspective acquaintance. Such a view would be implied by a certain theory of the self, namely that the self is nothing over and above the collection of its mental states; for then acquaintance with the self would just *be* acquaintance with the contents of the mind. But in order to avoid making the introspective theory of self-acquaintance depend upon the correctness of this controversial view of the self, let us formulate that theory after the pattern of the weaker thesis of the last paragraph: that is, the introspective theory will say that there exists some relation, of an acquaintance-transmitting sort, between the self and its mental states, and that accordingly acquaintance with the latter yields acquaintance with the former via that relation. This theory has the incidental advantage of suggesting an answer to an old worry about whether the self is encounterable in introspection. This worry, often supposed devastating to the idea of an introspectible self distinct from its mental states, is to the effect that the alleged self is not an item to be come across by inner inspection: we come across thoughts, feelings, sensations and so forth, but we never light upon the self which is supposed to be the subject of these – the bare self is introspectively unencounterable. At first sight this seems a powerful objection, but a comparison with the case of perceiving external objects casts some doubt on its cogency. For it appears equally true that when we perceive an external object we come across only its parts or surfaces or aspects; we never perceive the 'bare

substance' which is supposed to be the bearer of these directly perceptible features. So it is hard to see how someone could accept this line of
thought in the case of the self and reject it in the case of material
objects. In both cases, the introspective theorist will say, what makes
us allow that acquaintance with a self or material substance takes place
is that these objects are in certain acquaintance-transmitting relations
to the items conceded to be unproblematically accessible: namely that
the self *has* those immediately introspectible states, and that the
material substance *has* the parts or aspects through which it is presented to perception. What the introspective theory hopes to do, in
short, is to account for self-acquaintance on the model of the mediate
objects of perception, with mental states serving as the mediators.
Such a theory, if correct, would remove much of the mystery surrounding the topic of self-awareness. But the theory looks suspect –
the self resists being cast in the role of mediate object of introspection.
Can we spell out the unease the theory engenders?

We cannot refute this theory in the way we refuted the perceptual
theory, namely by conceiving cases of self-acquaintance which are not
mediated by the item claimed to be the basis of this sort of acquaintance, because, as we said earlier, it is not conceivable that someone
should be aware of himself and not be introspectively aware of his
mental states – we therefore cannot peel the introspective basis away
and leave self-acquaintance intact. But equally, we said, it is not
possible to be introspectively aware and not self-aware; and this provides the clue to why the introspective theory is unacceptable. The
intuition to work with is that awareness of self is just as fundamental as
awareness of one's own mental states; it is not something we can regard
as *derivative* from that awareness. It would not do to put this simply by
saying that you cannot have acquaintance with the contents of your
mind without having awareness of the self whose mind it is, since it is
also true that you cannot perceive the parts composing an external
object without perceiving the object – this on its own does not undermine the claim of derivativeness. But a small adjustment in this
formulation of the objection does give a genuine asymmetry between
the cases: we can readily imagine perceiving a mediating item (a part,
say) without perceiving the object perception of which that item
mediates if we *detach* the former from the latter; but we cannot
perform such detachment or abstraction in the case of mental states
and the self. Thus we can separate the branches from a tree and so
perceive the branches without perceiving the tree of which they were
parts; but there is no sense in the idea of separating mental states from
the self and being aware of them in isolation. Since the notion of

perceptual derivativeness appears to depend upon such contingent relations between mediate and the immediate perceptual objects, and since these sorts of relation do not obtain in respect of the self and its mental states, the introspective theory seems to rest critically upon a false presupposition. And this suggests that self-awareness is a primitive species of acquaintance not assimilable to ordinary introspection. In a sense, then, it turns out that there was something right in the thought that the self is unencounterable: for if it *were* introspectible it would have to be so *un*derivatively, since this appears to be the sort of acquaintance with the self that we have; but since there is no *immediate* introspection of the self, the self cannot be an introspectible object at all. This implies that, after all, there is more force to the claim that the self is unencounterable than to the claim that material substances are unencounterable: the latter claim is resistable by invoking the idea of transferred perception, but the former cannot be disarmed in an analogous way. In short, acquaintance with the self is not just a matter of ordinary (relatively) unproblematic introspective acquaintance, but something *sui generis*. Can we say anything more positive about this mode of acquaintance, though?

At this point two options present themselves: seeing that acquaintance with the self is not explicable in terms of either perceptual or introspective acquaintance, we might become sceptical about the whole idea of such a peculiar kind of acquaintance, perhaps even inferring that the self is a chimera; or we might resolutely accept that there is this special *sui generis* acquaintance, however philosophically perplexing it might appear. The first option does away with the problem by declaring that there *is* no primitive mental act of self-awareness to concern ourselves over; assessing this radical line requires discussion of the nature of the self, a topic we must defer till later. Let us for the moment proceed on the assumption that we are dealing with a genuine mental act whose object is the self and enquire as to its nature in an uncritical spirit. Then we have our usual questions: What is the character of the mode of presentation of a self? How does this mode of presentation relate to the object of such acquaintance? What is the nature of the dyadic relation involved – in particular, does the self cause the mental act of acquaintance with it? These are obscure questions, and any answer to them must be fraught with doubt; nevertheless something may be said about them.

Presumably the mode of presentation of a self must have some representational content: is this general in character, and does it uniquely identify the self that is presented? A natural answer is that there is a sense in which each self is presented to itself in the same way:

when someone thinks 'I am thus-and-so' he thinks of himself as an object of the same type as others capable of such thoughts; indeed the constant meaning of the word 'I' on different lips suggests as much. If, *per impossibile*, your self were presented to me from a first-person point of view, then I would think of that self in the same way as I think about the self with which I am actually presented. Or if my self kept changing its identity over time, so that numerically distinct selves occupied my body, then I would think of each self in the same way. (These suppositions are, of course, absurd, but they may help to bring out the generality that seems present in the way selves are presented to themselves.) An analogy that may be helpful here is the concept of the *present*: different times can be given as present – as when we refer to successive times as 'now'. Each of these times is given in the same way, as *the present*; so there is a sense in which the mode of presentation associated with uses of 'now' is general. If we conceive 'I' on the model of 'now', we can similarly see that the mode of presentation associated with different uses of 'I' by different selves is uniform. Given this, it follows that modes of self-presentation will not uniquely determine *which* self is presented – content does not determine object. This failure of determination might be made vivid by considering two selves alike in every respect, in particular psychologically indistinguishable: when they use 'I' what is going on in their minds is exactly the same. It seems then that they are presented to themselves in precisely the same way, though the objects presented – what 'I' refers to in each of their mouths – are distinct. This is shown in the fact that the psychological significance of the mental acts involved is the same in both cases: they will be disposed to act in the same way on the basis of the thoughts they have about themselves. In this respect the content of self-awareness is logically parallel to the content of perceptual and introspective awareness.

If the content of acts of self-awareness does not determine their object, then, as with the other cases we have discussed, we need some other factor to explain why this object rather than that is the one with which the subject is acquainted: we need something to determine that it is *this* self that I am aware of. Here the appeal to causal connections looks distinctly unpromising: it seems absurd to suggest that the self causes acquaintance with itself. Partly this is because the self and awareness of it are too close together: we cannot conceive of self-awareness – a mental act whose content is as of a self of such and such a sort – in the absence of the self to which it is directed. As with introspection, we cannot make sense of anything like an *hallucination* of the self; so again, no problem of non-standard causal connections could arise in respect of a self and an act of awareness as of a self. This is not to deny that the self and an act of acquaintance with it are distinct items; but they do not seem related in such a way that the former might cause the latter – still less that causal relations could furnish the complete explanation of the relation of acquaintance with the self. Indeed, it seems in this case that the only answer we can give to the question is this: it is this self rather than that which is the object of a given act of self-awareness just because it is this self rather than that whose act of awareness *it is*. Nothing further needs to be added to the information that a given self has a mental act as of a self presented under 'I' to determine *which* self is thus presented. This makes the case of self-acquaintance essentially different from both perceptual and introspective acquaintance. Whether anything further can be said to characterise the relation of acquaintance as it holds between a given self and that same self remains moot. But on this indecisive note we shall leave the topic of acquaintance with the self.

We have made a point, in this chapter, of discussing several varieties of acquaintance, with a view to determining whether they are susceptible of a uniform account. We have found that there are some significant parallels between the different varieties, especially as regards their abstract structure. But we have also been led to conclude that there are equally significant dissimilarities, notably as to the nature of the relational aspect. The moral to be drawn is that any adequate theory of acquaintance must address itself to the different species of acquaintance, and be prepared to discover that no perfectly general theory is to be had. There seems to be no one way in which the mind gets directed on to reality.

4 Thought and language

Normal human beings are gifted with both mind and language: in particular, they have thoughts which get expressed in speech. But how intimate is the connection between possessing a mind and operating a language? Can we shear language off and leave mental phenomena intact beneath, or is it rather that the capacity to speak informs the mind, so that subtracting language would involve removing the mind? Is language merely the contingent manifestation of thought, required only for the communication of thoughts to others, or should we say that language is the stuff of thought, its necessary vehicle? These are the questions with which we shall deal in the present chapter.

While the dependence of mind on language is a matter of dispute and difficulty, the converse dependence is not generally supposed to be. Thus it appears evident that speaking a language requires the possession of thoughts, these being precisely what the sentences of a language express. This supposition needs a qualification, however, in view of the signal systems exploited by certain animals to which we would be reluctant to ascribe thoughts – for example, bees and termites. These systems of communication are sufficiently like language to make it worth declaring them an exception to the dependence of language on thought: they are complex and structured, and it does not seem wrong to evaluate the messages their symbols convey for truth and falsity, or at least for correctness and incorrectness. But a significant difference from language proper is that the creatures operating these signal systems do not plausibly make *assertions* in producing communicative messages; for assertion does require a foundation of propositional attitudes. So we should say, more strictly, that performing speech acts such as assertion presupposes the possession of mind.

We should also make it quite explicit that we are concerned with the relation between *propositional attitudes* and language, not mental phenomena in general. It is obvious enough that sensations do not depend on language for their enjoyment: creatures can suffer pain without being able to say so. Perception too should be allowed to the non-linguistic: a creature can surely see a predator or taste grass in the absence of language – and the experiences involved must have informational content of some sort. Since these mental phenomena clearly do not depend upon linguistic ability, we can say that the possession of consciousness is not necessarily bound up with language: the experiential or phenomenological is not internally connected with language. Where the connection begins to look more constitutive is with mental states directed on to *propositions*: propositions are what sentences express, and it is tempting to suppose that a mind cannot get directed on to propositions except via the sentences which express them. Thus it has appeared natural to many to take seriously the idea that 'we think in words', words being what enable us to think propositionally.

This question as to whether thought is essentially linguistic has, we may parenthetically note, a significance which goes beyond getting clear on the nature of thinking: for on its resolution turns the larger question of what philosophy should conceive itself as studying. Philosophy, we may say, is principally concerned to investigate the means by which we represent the world. But is this means of representation essentially linguistic or is it not? Well, we can agree that we represent reality in thought, through the exercise of concepts. So if it should turn out that thinking consists in the deployment of language, then it would seem that philosophy should address itself to language; the philosophy of language thus becomes the fulcrum of philosophy, its fundamental object of study. But if we should conclude that thought and language are separable, in such a way that the latter cannot explain the former, then in studying the structure of thought we should not really be studying language – or not essentially. This would dethrone philosophy of language from its alleged position of pre-eminence, or at least its title to centrality would have to be otherwise established. It would then seem that the philosophy of *mind* becomes central, because the question as to the general nature of thought, in particular how thought contrives to represent reality, is a question within the philosophy of mind (we come back to this issue in the Epilogue).

In order to sharpen our enquiry into manageable form we shall consider a quite precise theory of thought or judgement which is of some historical and contemporary importance; we shall label this theory the 'inner saying' theory. Let us begin by stating the theory in a forthright way, and then proceed to assess its advantages and difficulties. What the inner saying theory claims is that to judge, for example, that snow is white, that is, to have that thought, precisely *is* to execute a mental utterance of a sentence expressing the proposition that snow is white. That is, to make a judgement is to stand in a certain psychological relation to an interior linguistic item – to employ, in a word, a language of thought. Thus, just as the outer assertion that snow is white consists in a relation to a sentence which means that snow is white, so to judge inwardly that snow is white is to be internally related to a sentence endowed with that meaning. We may accordingly analyse judgement into two elements, on the inner saying theory: first, a relation of mentally uttering between judger and inner sentence; and second, the circumstance that the inner sentence has a certain semantic content. According to this theory, we think in words in a perfectly literal sense, as literal as the sense in which we speak in words: sentences are the vehicle of inner thought just as they are the vehicle of communicative speech.

Various questions can be raised about the identity and origin of the language of thought, which we shall briefly mention but not pursue, since they are somewhat tangential to our main theme. We can ask, first, whether the inner language is identical with the thinker's public language – is Giovanni's language of thought simply Italian? If there is this identity, then we can expect to obtain a theory of someone's language of thought by devoloping a theory of his spoken language, these having the same grammar and vocabulary. But if Giovanni's inner language is not a natural language but a special language hitherto undeciphered and undescribed, then we would need to devise ways of gaining access to this covert language – and we may discover that it differs radically from the spoken language. Secondly, and connectedly, we can ask whether a thinker's inner language is shared by all human beings or indeed by all conceivable thinkers: that is, is there a universal language of thought? Some have supposed that thought proceeds in an ideal language free of the blemishes that disfigure the language we speak; in days past it was Latin that was taken as the model for this ideal universal language, nowadays it tends to be the predicate calculus. And thirdly we can ask, again connectedly, whether the language of thought is innate or learned: are the syntax and semantics of a person's inner language programmed into his genes, or is it that the child acquires his language of thought by listening to adults, or perhaps in some other way? Depending upon how we choose to answer these questions, we get two extreme positions: at one extreme is the suggestion that all thinkers employ the same innately universal language whose properties we are pretty much ignorant of; at the other extreme is the suggestion that each thinker employs his own idiosyncratic language of thought, this coinciding with the acquired language he speaks. In what follows we shall try not to presuppose either of these positions; to fix ideas, however, the reader is invited to suppose that his inner judgements are executed in his ordinary spoken language.

One way to test a theory is to ask what it would explain if it were true: if the theory can account for facts we acknowledge independently of subscription to the theory, then the theory is to that extent confirmed. Let us then try to find features of thought which would be explained by the supposition that judging is inner saying; or equivalently, let us see what the inner saying theory predicts about thought and ask whether these predictions are correct.

An important feature of thoughts is that they have structure, specifically logical structure. Thus we have compound thoughts, for example thinking that snow is white and coal is black; thoughts involving multiple generality, for example the thought that everyone loves someone who hates himself; modal thoughts like the thought that necessarily $7 + 5 = 12$: in fact we can specify thoughts of any structure represented in language, simply by completing 'X judges that . . .' with an arbitrary declarative sentence. This structure on the part of our judgements confers a capacity to have infinitely many thoughts, since elements in the structure can be recombined to yield indefinitely many distinct thoughts: judgements have what is sometimes called a recursive structure, in that they involve devices which may be repeated at will to generate infinitely many potential thoughts. It is this structure that permits a finite creature to wield such an infinite capacity: our capacity to make judgements of arbitrary complexity rests upon a finite basis of capacities relating to elements of the structure. Any theory of judgement, therefore, must represent this capacity as a finitely based structured ability. Integrally connected with this property of structure is the potential novelty of thoughts – the ability to make new judgements on the basis of old abilities. Indefinitely many states of affairs may be presented to a thinker, and among these will be states of affairs he has never encountered before: yet he will be able to make appropriate judgements about those hitherto unencountered states of affairs, and he will do this novel thing on the basis of a mastery of elements of a recombinable structure. Furthermore, it is the possession of structure that makes it possible for thoughts to figure as they do in trains of reasoning: in reasoning we pass from one judgement to another on the strength of the logical relations between judgements induced by their structure. Reasoning is a psychological capacity whose structure must mirror the structure of the propositions with which the reasoning is concerned. So in all these ways – finite basis, novelty, reasoning – judgements are shown to be structured; indeed, their structure must recapitulate the structure of sentences in language. Language for its part must be accorded structure for similar sorts of reasons: to explain how the capacity to understand a language can encompass infinitely many sentences upon a finite base; to account for the ability to understand and produce novel sentences; and to represent the logical relations between sentences. And there is, in fact, a considerable body of theory about language which attempts to do justice to these features of language and our understanding of it. Given all this it is very natural to suggest that the structural features of thought which parallel these features of language do so precisely because they are strictly derivative from those features: thoughts have structure *because* they involve relations to structured sentences. Thus the structure of a thought just is the structure of some internal sentence; and so a theory of the structure of language will carry over directly to the structure of propositional attitudes. We can then say that for a concept to be exercised in a judgement is for some internal word to be a constituent of an appropriate internal sentence; and the role of a concept in contributing to a judgement will be the same as the role of a word in contributing toward the meaning of a sentence – whatever our theory of the latter role may be. So the inner saying theory seems to offer an *explanation* of the structure of thoughts.

A second advantage that might be claimed for the inner saying theory is that it provides us with a *medium* of thought. Suppose we say, as seems natural, that thinking involves internal representations of the world thought about: then we will have the question what is the medium of this representation. If we suppose thinking to be done in words, then we have a ready answer to this question: the representational medium is linguistic. Thus, just as we can investigate the medium of communication – the marks and sounds that carry meaning – so we could in principle investigate the linguistic medium of thought, perhaps by ascertaining the properties of the informational code the brain uses. The inner saying theory promises to supply an account of what is going on in the head when a person thinks.

The theory also helps to unify and simplify the analysis of *reports* of acts of judgement and of speech. In reported speech we aim to produce a sentence, embedded in 'X said that . . .', which matches in purport the content of the utterance made by the subject of the report; and our report is true or false according as we do or do not succeed in using a sentence matching the content of the subject's sentence. Now reports of thoughts are logically very similar to reports of speech; we are likewise trying to represent the world in the way the subject does. It would be pleasing, theoretically, to be able to view both sorts of report as variations on the same theme, so that a uniform analysis could be given. And this we are enabled to do by the inner saying theory: a report of someone's judgement will be correct if the embedded sentence used in the report matches the content of the inwardly uttered sentence of the judger's language of thought. The theory thus explains the similarity between the two sorts of report.

There is another similarity between thought and language that the inner saying theory might claim to explain: this is that both thought and language exhibit a certain kind of *holism*. Thus it is not implausible to suggest that thoughts do not have their content in isolation – to have one thought is to have many others conceptually and evidentially connected with the given one. In consequence, we cannot really make sense of the idea of a creature possessed of but a single thought; moreover, when we ascribe a thought to a creature we are implicitly ascribing a whole network of further thoughts. But it is also plausible to suggest that the meaning and mastery of sentences is similarly holistic: sentences do not have meaning in isolation, and we understand a given sentence in the context of others with which it is semantically connected. In consequence, we cannot make sense of a speaker whose understanding is restricted to a single sentence; and when we interpret someone's uttered word we are implicitly interpreting other words of his. Now if such holism is accepted, whatever its strength may be, we can ask why it characterises both thought and language; and the inner saying theory has an answer – because thought just consists in the manipulation of inner sentences and these are holistic as to content.

Finally, the theory promises a uniform account of what it is that confers a particular content. We can ask in virtue of what a judgement is about some item in the world, and we can ask what determines the psychological role of a judgement. We can similarly ask what it is that confers a certain semantic content on a sentence. On the inner saying theory, we can take the aboutness of judgements to be a special case of reference: my thought is about Jones just if the corresponding inner sentence contains a word which denotes Jones; and for me to ascribe a concept to something in judgement is for me to perform an act of mental word predication. The psychological role of a thought will, likewise, be determined by the psychological role of an appropriate sentence – where this might perhaps be characterised in terms of propensities to accept or reject sentences under various sorts of evidential conditions. About the world-directed aspect of thought content, then, we shall say that any adequate theory of reference will constitute a theory of it: acquaintance with things thus gets explained as consisting in the reference of inner words. The theses we enunciated in Chapter 3 regarding content and its relation to the object of acquaintance then come out as special cases of the relation between sense and reference – the relation, namely, between what a word signifies to someone and the object it stands for. On this way of looking at the matter, it will be a prior causal account of the reference relation which underlies the causal nature of the link between the mental act of thinking about an external object and the object thought about.

None of these considerations amounts to a direct argument for the inner saying theory, but taken together they look a fairly impressive set of reasons for finding the theory attractive. However, a theory can look appealing in its capacity to account for the data and still not stand up to critical scrutiny; so let us now survey some of the problems a captious critic might raise. We can divide the objections into two main groups: those that deny that judging can be compared to inner saying, and those that issue from the claim that there can be thought without language. The first group of objections can be presented in three parts: (i) objections to the effect that the verb used to analyse 'judge', namely 'say', is conceptually inappropriate; (ii) the denial that judgements have their content in the same way sentences do; and (iii) allegations of circularity in the theory. Let us consider these three objections in turn.

The inner saying theory holds that thinking is a kind of speech act, performed internally. Now speech acts are, precisely, *acts* – things you do intentionally. But can it be right to suggest that an episode of thinking is an intentional action? Suppose a black cat passes by and you have the thought 'There goes a black cat': is it correct to say that your having that thought was something you did intentionally – that it was an upshot of *will*? The answer seems obviously to be that it is *not* correct, since making that judgement was forming a belief – and forming beliefs is something that comes over you rather than something you actively initiate. This involuntariness is clearest in the case of perceptual judgements: for perceiving an object is patently not an intentional action, and perceptual judging is a direct result of that. If judging were really a kind of action, then we would possess all our beliefs by choice, in just the way that we choose to perform our acts of speech: but plainly judging and saying are dissimilar in this respect. So it must be wrong to treat thinking as the performance of inner speech acts of saying. The wrongness is shown in the cogency of the claim that you cannot *decide* to believe a proposition: you cannot just straight out decide to believe that now it is sunny – especially if you know very well that it is raining. But the impossibility of deciding to believe presupposes that forming a belief is not an intentional action; for if it were you could decide to undertake it. On the inner saying theory, however, deciding to believe should be no more difficult that deciding to say. We might spell out the point as follows: what you believe is what you hold yourself to know, so that from the believer's point of view deciding to believe is deciding to know; but to have knowledge is (in part) for the world to be in conformity with your beliefs; so deciding to believe would involve deciding that the world be a certain way; but you cannot intelligibly decide that the world shall match your beliefs, because belief is the kind of mental state whose office it is to fit the world; so deciding to believe would require you both to know what kind of state belief is and not to know this – that is, to have an incoherent conception of belief. It is quite different with speech acts: to decide to assert something does not involve deciding to know it, but only deciding that the *hearer* shall know or believe what one asserts. From these considerations, therefore, it appears that the inner saying theory mischaracterises the relation of judging: it assigns judgement to the domain of the will, where it does not belong.

Another objection one may be tempted to make is that acts of speech are temporally extended sequences of events, whereas judging does not have this temporally successive character: we make a judgement all at once, so to speak, but saying takes time. This asymmetry is certainly present if we consider our usual methods of saying something; but it is not clear that we could not imagine a method of speech which reproduced the way in which the constituents of the content of a judgement are (if they are) simultaneously before the mind. Think, for example, of issuing one's speech acts with a sophisticated rubber stamp: this way of saying something would not have the temporally successive character of vocal speech or of left-to-right writing. Furthermore, we are familiar with the phenomenon of taking in whole sentences at a glance; so our understanding of speech acts need not be successive if their production is not. The inner saying theory thus seems capable of capturing this alleged feature of judgement.

A more worrying question is how the theory is to deal with propositional attitudes other than belief and its kin. In the case of belief there is a natural choice of speech act, since saying is the characteristic expression of belief; but what speech act corresponds to desire, say? It cannot be the speech act of command because you can desire something and not be prepared to command that it be brought about, and you can command something you do not yourself desire. The optative mood seems closer to what is wanted: to desire a coconut is to utter inwardly 'Would that I had a coconut!' But this raises the question of sincerity: for you can perform such a speech act *in*sincerely – you proclaim a desire for a coconut but in point of fact you do not have that desire. Shall we say that the inwardly uttered optative can be uttered insincerely or shall we deny this? If we say it can be, then we do not yet have an adequate theory of desire, since the performance of the internal speech act is not sufficient for the presence of the desire; and what seems to be missing in cases of insincerity is just the desire itself. But if we make inner speech acts necessarily sincere, hoping thereby to avoid the threat of circularity, then there is the question whether it can still be right to call these speech acts, since the possibility of insincerity seems essential to the idea of speech: in speech we represent ourselves as having various attitudes, and these representations may be deceptive. At the least the inner saying theory needs to do something to explain why the application of speech act verbs to inner linguistic actions does not entail the possibility of insincerity. But even if this could be explained there would still remain many kinds of propositional attitude for which there is no natural choice of corresponding speech act – hoping, fearing, expecting, doubting etc.

In response to these objections the theory might offer to give up the idea that judging is any kind of speech act. What is essential to the theory, it may be said, is the idea of inner sentences, not the claim that the thinker's relation to these sentences is that of *utterance*. We might, then, delete talk of inner *saying* and replace it with some less committal characterisation of how sentences feature in thought. But in what relation does the judger stand to the internal sentence if it is not the relation of uttering the sentence in a certain mode? Two replies suggest themselves: we could admit that there is no readily available *psychological* description of the relation, but suggest that we compare the manipulation of sentences in thought to the operations performed by computers on the sentences of the languages with which they are programmed; alternatively, we could use the psychological notion of accepting or assenting to an internal sentence, thus picturing the thinker as cast in the role of hearer rather than speaker. The first reply is suspect because the 'languages' used by computers are not languages in the ordinary and required sense: the computer does not *understand* the sentences it operates on, and printing out symbols on a tape is not a kind of assertion. It is necessary to the inner saying theory that it stay within the domain of interpreted and understood language; but then we shall need to be provided with some appropriate mentalistic description of the internal relation. The second possible reply raises troublesome questions about how someone could be in the position of hearer with respect to his own inner sentences: how can we conceive of the judger being somehow presented with internal sentences which he is invited to accept as true? Whence do the sentences come? Why is assent necessary at all if their source is himself? Can the thinker ever reject a sentence that is presented to him? These questions bring out the oddity of the idea of casting the thinker in the role of the recipient of sentences to which he is required to assent. The indicated conclusion, then, is that the inner saying theory cannot plausibly regard the internal relation as an act of mental utterance, but it is hard to preserve its perspicuity and appeal by trying to find some other description of how the thinker is to be related to his internal sentences: the best we can do is to say, lamely, that the sentences 'occur' in the person's mind, but we are unable to give this any real colour.

The second class of objections to the inner saying theory concerns the manner in which thoughts have content: do they have content in the way sentences do? Sentences have content in virtue of conventional semantic rules assigning a particular interpretation to each word of the sentence: for example, a particular object is assigned to a name as its reference. Consider a (public) utterance of the sentence 'That dog is noisy', and compare this with a judgement that that dog is noisy. How does the phrase 'that dog' achieve its reference to a particular dog? It does so by virtue of conventional rules relating the utterance to its context, usually implicating some gesture such as pointing at the said noisy dog. But when you judge that that dog is noisy this judgement is directed on to the dog in virtue of different mechanisms: it will involve attending to some perceptually presented dog, and attending to something given in perception is not to be construed as the following of conventional rules which determine something as a reference. It thus seems wrong to say that such judgements involve the learning and deployment of certain conventions; they are more primitive than that, being tied to perception. This objection is reinforced by the consideration that while there is an essential *arbitrariness* in the nature of language, this is not so for thought: which language you speak is arbitrary in the sense that you could have spoken another to the same effect; but it sounds wrong to suggest that how we think is arbitrary in this way, since thinking is the exercise of *concepts*, and these are not conventional and arbitrary in the way words are. This intuitive difference between language and thought is perhaps what explains the desire, on the part of some proponents of the language of thought hypothesis, to hold that the inner language is not conventional in nature but is somehow *natural*: that its symbols are not arbitrarily linked with what they signify but are somehow naturally dictated by the nature of the things they apply to. But this is not credible, because it is in the nature of language to be conventional: so the inclination to deny that the language of thought is conventional must really stem from recognition that thought is not properly linguistic – that thoughts are not constituted by words.

There is another respect in which thought content differs from sentence content: this is that the meaning of a sentence depends upon facts about the community of speakers in a way that the content of someone's thought does not depend upon the community of thinkers. Because the meaning of a sentence is public property, a person can utter a sentence whose meaning he does not grasp and it nevertheless be true that the sentence had its public meaning on his lips – the words do not lose their meaning just because the speaker does not understand them. But this property of sentence content does not seem to apply, or not to the same degree, to the content of thoughts – you cannot think a proposition you do not grasp. But if judging were mentally uttering a sentence with a meaning, then there should be no such restriction on what can be thought: you could succeed in thinking that sesquipedali-anism is an affliction of the erudite just by inwardly uttering that sentence, despite the fact that these words mean nothing to you. So saying something with a content can be dependent on being part of a language community in which words have a public meaning, but you cannot expect your thoughts to have content just by internally uttering words you correctly believe to have a content but whose content you do not grasp. The existence of malapropism demonstrates this difference vividly: malapropism occurs in speech when a person's intended meaning does not match the words he chooses to express that meaning; but there can be no such mismatch in thought, since there is nothing with public content to come apart from private meaning. To make a judgement with a determinate content one needs actually to *have* the concepts involved in the judgement; but to say something with a definite content this is not necessary.

These differences between the two sorts of content do not perhaps decisively refute the inner saying theory, since they could be disputed or held inessential; but they do raise real questions about the theory that need convincing rebuttals if the theory is to deserve credence. It will help put these objections in a clearer light if we turn to the third sort of objection we mentioned, namely allegations of circularity; for the import of this sort of objection is that the inner saying theory seems able to capture some of the central features of thought only because it is circular – that is, it uses the distinctive features of thought to explain themselves, while taking an idle detour through language. The charge of circularity is, in a nutshell, this: language can seem to explain thought only because speech is to be understood as the *expression* of thought. Thus suppose you hear the speech of a foreigner whose language you do not understand: you assume that he is giving expression to a thought which gives his words content. Without this assumption, it seems, his utterance would be mere sound, devoid of significance. But now what of the underlying thought itself? If we analyse this as an inner speech act, then it seems that the conjectured internal utterance must in turn express some thought if it is not to be just a collection of unmeaning characters: but of course this launches us on an infinite regress. The objector is confronting the inner saying theory with a dilemma: either we say that the inner sentence expresses a thought, in which case the theory is circular; or it does not express a thought, in which case it can have no semantic content. The suggestion is that outer speech has meaning by being connected with propositional attitudes, so we cannot hope to explain what it is to have a propositional attitude by claiming that attitudes consist in inner speech. This objection does not, as stated, deny that when we think we inwardly utter; what it denies is that such inner utterance could *explain* what it is to think contentful thoughts. And if the inner saying theory can no longer be regarded as explanatory, the motivation lapses for insisting that we recognise the existence of a language of thought.

It might be suggested, as a way of meeting this objection, that we claim a difference in the way outer and inner speech acquire significance. Thus we might concede that outer speech has content because it is expressive of thought, but deny that inner speech has content in this way; we hold that it has content in a more basic way. The idea will be that judgement involves a relation to a sentence with meaning, but its having that meaning does not come from expressing a thought – this is a matter of prior interpretative facts. These more basic facts may include relations of reference and determinants of psychological role; when these are combined with a relation of inward utterance we get a thought – but not before. The picture, then, is that the inner sentences are the basic objects of interpretation; their content confers content upon thoughts; and thoughts transmit their content to outer speech. However, this manoeuvre does not evade the fundamental objection, even if the picture it recommends is granted. For there now rises up a new dilemma, naturally descended from the first: either the inner sentences have their content determined by facts which go beyond their merely formal properties, in which case *these* facts will be what really constitute the content of thoughts; or else we shall try to get by, theoretically, just with the sentences – but then won't they be just meaningless bits of syntax? The second horn of this dilemma points out that no system of linguistic signs can ever be, so to say, self-interpreting, and so the inner saying theory needs to introduce resources capable of conferring significance on the internal sentences; the first horn asserts that such extra resources will render the internal sentences themselves theoretically superfluous – we could simply drop the sentences and let the conditions that are brought in to interpret them do all the work. At the least, it will be these additional resources, whatever they may be, that will be ultimately accounting for the features of thought that the inner saying theory was designed to capture. The attraction of the inner saying theory was that it promised to explain judgement in terms of mere words, but closer inspection has shown this suggestion to be spurious. We could put the point, very simply, as follows: everyone can agree that judgement is the exercise of concepts – we think 'in' concepts; the inner saying theory offers an account of what this exercise of concepts consists in – it consists in the internal manipulation of words; but words have content only because they express concepts; so the theory presupposes what it set out to explain. To fulfil its ambition, therefore, the inner saying theory must tell us what it is for an inner word to express a particular concept; but then the threat is that this account of concepts, which cannot make appeal to the meaning of words, will make the imputation of a language of thought theoretically redundant, since a concept will presumably consist in some kind of non-linguistic internal representation capable of doing all the jobs inner words were cut out to do.

The only way of avoiding the consequent extrusion of language from the theory of thought would be to claim that possessing a concept precisely consists in the inner employment of words: that is, to propose a sort of dispositional analysis of concept-possession in which words are held to be essentially involved in the exercise of the disposition. The main trouble with this suggestion is that it suffers from the defects of all dispositional analyses of mental phenomena: it takes the dispositional upshot of a mental state to exhaust the intrinsic nature of the state. As we saw in Chapter 2, we should rather say that dispositions are had *in virtue of* intrinsic properties; but then what is the nature of the *intrinsic* property corresponding to the disposition to employ words inwardly? When we are told the answer to this question, the claim will then be that the disposition to use the word *issues from* this prior intrinsic property, and so again words will fall away as inessential to the constitution of thoughts.

But there is a further line of objection to the linguistic theory of concept-possession that is part and parcel of the inner saying theory of thought, and this is the claim that it is possible for a creature to have concepts and have no language. The denial of this – the thesis that no creature could think unless it also spoke – is weaker than the thesis that thinking is inward saying, since plainly the first thesis might be true for reasons independent of the truth of the second. But it seems evident enough that the second implies the first: if thinking is conducted in language, then there can be no thinking where there is not speech or at least the capacity for speech. This entailment is not quite strict, however, since the claim that thinking involves *inner* speech does not immediately commit us to holding that thought is possible only for those gifted with *outer* speech: but it would be a desperate ploy to use this logical gap to fend off the objection from the claim that thought is possible in the absence of linguistic ability. It could scarcely be plausibly maintained that dogs (say), though they never utter a word, are nevertheless internally loquacious. Let us then take it that the thesis that thought requires speech is indeed weaker than the inner saying theory, so that the fate of the former determines that of the latter. We shall turn now to that thesis; we shall find that it is by no means easy to decide upon its correctness.

The question whether there can be thought without language is vulgarly put by asking whether animals have beliefs. This is a bad way to put the question, for two (connected) reasons. In the first place it misleadingly suggests that we are asking a question of empirical fact about the various animals (pets, it generally turns out) that inhabit the earth, a question which it seems appropriate to answer by careful observation of these animals' behaviour. But of course we are supposed to be asking a conceptual question: is it a conceptually necessary truth that thought is possible only where there is language? And to answer this question we need an a priori conceptual investigation of the essential nature of thought and speech. Secondly, if we focus our attentions on the animals around us, we run the risk of misdiagnosing the source of their thoughtlessness – if we decide they are thoughtless – because our unwillingness to ascribe thoughts to them might be based upon some deficiency of ability which is quite independent of their linguistic incompetence – truncated attention span, poor memory, general lack of intelligence, etc. To formulate our question adequately we need to imagine a creature possessed of any abilities save those that clearly require the possession of language – and whether any actual animals meet these specifications is neither here nor there. Approaching the question in this more abstract way also prevents us being sidetracked with questions about whether various actual animals have a rudimentary language. Let us also be clear that the question is not whether speechless creatures can solve problems or process information; the question is whether they can have *propositional* attitudes, centrally the attitude of thought. So we must always be sure, when we find ourselves prepared to make a psychological ascription to a creature, that what we are prepared to ascribe is something of the form 'X thinks *that* such and such.'

The spontaneous verdict people are apt to give on this question is that it *is* perfectly possible to have thought without language. Two sources of this intuitive verdict may be conjectured, one deriving from the first-person perspective we have on our thoughts, the other relying on a point about our ascription of thoughts to others. The first of these is simply the knowledge we have that our thoughts can go unsaid: you can have a particular belief for decades and never express it in speech – so why should it be impossible that *all* of a creature's thoughts should go thus unsaid? We feel that we know what it would be like to be such a creature, and so we naturally feel that such a creature is possible. The second point is that we are familiar with cases in which we ascribe a thought to someone on the strength of his non-linguistic behaviour, this ascription being just as well founded – sometimes more so – as ascriptions on the basis of speech. And again, if it is possible for us to manifest our thoughts non-linguistically, then why should there not be a creature whose *sole* mode of thought expression was non-linguistic? In view of these two points, it seems fair to say that the onus of proof is on the person who wishes to deny that a creature can have thoughts yet lack the gift of speech. So what arguments might be marshalled to overturn the spontaneous verdict?

One line of argument takes an epistemological form: it suggests that we cannot really *know* what someone else believes unless we know what he says. Thus it is claimed that non-linguistic behaviour always leaves open a number of distinct ascriptions of belief, but sincere speech tells us exactly what someone believes. When we are unsure what someone is thinking we ask him, and this seems to settle the question. Deprived of this mode of access we would, it is argued, never be sure what thoughts a creature has; so we could not *know* the thoughts of a speechless creature. There are a number of points to make about this epistemological line of argument. First, the argument is 'verificationist' in form: it goes from considerations governing our *knowledge* of thoughts to a conclusion about the conditions for the possibility of there *being* thoughts. This verificationist way of arguing is not generally valid: it would obviously be wrong to argue that there cannot be electrons without measuring instruments on the ground that we can know about electrons only by observing measuring instruments. So, similarly, we might reply to the epistemological argument that it does not follow from the fact that we could never conclusively ascertain the thoughts of speechless creatures that they could not *have* any. Compare sensations: we would not think that the fact that our only sure way of knowing what sensations a person has is by asking him shows that it is impossible to have sensations without language.

Perhaps speech is the only sure indication of thought, but it does not follow that the possession of thought requires language. Furthermore, this line of argument expects too much in the way of evidence about the states of mind of others: so long as we can have *some* non-linguistic evidence of thought, we can give reasons why the ascription of thoughts to speechless creatures is justified – the evidence need not be conclusive. Second, it is a mistake to move from the conditions of the ascription of thoughts to creatures *with* speech to conclusions about their ascription to creatures *without* speech. It may be that when a creature has speech we take what it says to be the final arbiter of what it believes, but this does nothing to show that speech is needed when the creature does not talk. Speech may become the central mode of manifestation of thought when it is present, but in its absence other criteria may come into their own: a creature without speech will, it may be supposed, develop other ways of manifesting and conveying its thoughts. But third, and most fundamental, the epistemological argument takes a naïve view of speech and its interpretation. This failing comes out in two ways. One is that it is necessary, in order to guarantee the epistemological primacy of speech, to require that the person speak *sincerely*; but of course insincerity is not evident in linguistic behaviour – or else deception would be a lot harder than it is. To know whether someone speaks sincerely you have to know a good deal about his beliefs and desires – precisely the things that speech was supposed to put us infallibly on to. So the requirement of sincerity assumes that we can know at least some of a person's propositional attitudes *before* we know enough about his speech to use it in the ascription of a particular thought: to know that someone's utterance of 'Politicians are incorruptible' is sincere we have to know, in the limit, that he *believes* that politicians are incorruptible. But, it may be replied, to know this we need precisely to know the meaning of the uttered sentence; so we are still relying on language to get at belief, even if we admit that the sincerity condition requires that mere knowledge of sentence meaning be supplemented with ascriptions of appropriate propositional attitudes. But – and this is the second point – we cannot assume that sentence meaning itself is given to us directly: for speech itself has to be interpreted before it can afford glimpses of the speaker's thoughts (just consider the speech of foreigners). What this brings out is that speech interpretation is really just as conjectural as thought ascription; indeed, it is hard to see how meaning could be ascribed to someone's words without propositional attitudes being ascribed to him at the same time. We should see a person's linguistic and non-linguistic behaviour as *both* in need of interpretation; and interpreting one sort of behaviour will involve interpreting the other sort. Meaning and thought are thus both equally matters of conjecture; it is not that meaning is given and thought hidden. But if meaning is not immediately given, then we cannot take it to provide sure and prior access to thought; so there is not the asymmetry between linguistic and non-linguistic behaviour, in point of their capacity to reveal thought, that the epistemological argument relied upon. Speech seemed a better guide to thought than other sorts of behaviour only because we uncritically took its interpretation as given; but once we see that this assumption is naïve the appearance of asymmetry vanishes. Since speech cannot be taken as the *foundation* of thought ascription, there is no longer any argument for the claim that the only sure route to knowledge of a creature's thought is absent in the case of the speechless. When neither is assumed to be interpreted non-linguistic behaviour is at least as good as linguistic in warranting ascriptions of thought. For these reasons, then, the epistemological argument fails.

Another, quite different, way of attempting to demonstrate that thought requires language is to argue that having thoughts depends upon the possession of *other* capacities which themselves can be seen to require language. Thus consider the connection between thinking and rationality: if making judgements requires the ability to reason, and if the ability to reason requires subjection to normative standards of rationality, and if rationality requires self-consciousness – why then surely thought requires language, because self-consciousness does. The strategy here is to argue that having beliefs rests upon seemingly more sophisticated capacities which cannot be possessed independently of linguistic ability. This strategy seems to have some force when addressed to the question whether particular animals have beliefs, because we are rightly reluctant to attribute self-consciousness to (say) dogs – and so their lack of language is claimed to explain the difference between them and us in this respect. But this style of argument is unsatisfactory: first, because it does nothing to justify its last step – it simply invites us to agree that self-consciousness requires language; and second, even if we did agree to this, no *explanation* has yet been given as to why this connection holds – it remains at the level of brute intuition. The same sort of weakness blunts the following train of argument, which again seeks to build up the having of thoughts into something more sophisticated than we might have supposed. Suppose we agree, perhaps on the basis of the previous argument, that to have beliefs you must have the *concept* of belief. To have the concept of belief, the argument continues, you must be capable of *ascribing* beliefs, both to yourself and to others, since there is no possessing a concept without being able to use it. Ascribing beliefs is carried out in the context of a general psychological theory which systematically explains behaviour. So having the concept of belief requires that you be an interpreter of the behaviour of others; and since having beliefs requires having the concept of belief, it follows that no creature can be a thinker unless it is also an interpreter of behaviour. This line of reasoning is not implausible, but it fails to prove that thought requires language; for, again, we have been given no reason to agree that to be an interpreter of the behaviour of others you need to be a *speaker*. Nothing has been said to exclude the possibility that your interpreting psychological ascriptions proceed wholly in your inner judgements about others' behaviour – you simply have thoughts about the thoughts of others. So even if we intuitively feel that the sophisticated capacity with which thinking has been connected does somehow depend upon linguistic ability, we have not yet explained or justified this feeling.

A third attempt to link thought with language looks more promising: it insists that without language there is nothing for the distinctions of content among thoughts to consist in. This argument may be formulated epistemologically as the thesis that we cannot make fine discriminations in our ascriptions of thoughts unless we can appeal to the meanings of words spoken by the thinkers in question; but the argument should really be seen as a constitutive one – it says that only distinctions of meaning in the words a person utters can constitute the distinctions of content we acknowledge in thoughts. Thus we might wonder what it would be for a dog to think that his master is at the door rather than that the man who takes him for a walk is about to enter 23 Lyndhurst Avenue. We know what this distinction of content comes to for those with speech – namely, a preparedness to produce or assent to the corresponding sentences – but it is unclear that there is anything for the distinction to consist in for the speechless. The question being pressed here is what account can be given of what it is to possess one concept rather than another if we do not have words to fall back on. Two retorts may be made to this question. First, it does not show that *simple* thoughts, coarse-grained in their content, require language – for example, the thought that it is cold or that danger is near; so it would only be sophisticated thoughts that need language. Second, the argument is uncritical about distinctions of meaning: as with the epistemological argument, we cannot just assume that facts about meaning are given while facts about thought call for explication. So it is fair to ask what distinctions of *meaning* are to consist in; and it is natural to reply that they consist in the expression of distinct *concepts*.

But if distinctions of meaning consist in distinctions in the concepts associated with words, then we cannot claim to have given thought content a *basis* in meaning. The question at issue here is this: do words have their meaning in virtue of the concepts people associate with them, or is it that people have the concepts they have in virtue of the words they understand? This is a very difficult question: on the one hand, it looks plausible to suggest that complex and refined concepts can enter a person's thought only through the medium of a language; but on the other, it seems that concepts *must* be logically prior to meanings. The reason this latter thing seems true is that words can only have semantic life breathed into them if people take them to express certain concepts, and a word can be understood by someone only if he has the conceptual resources to grasp its meaning. It is sometimes said that we can make all this intelligible by supposing that simple concepts can give rise to words expressing those concepts, but that once words are to hand (or mind) they have the capacity to beget further concepts. Now as a matter of natural psychological history this seems right enough, but it should really strike us as something of a mystery – for how could a mere mark or sound magically bestow a concept on someone? The process of acquiring new concepts is hardly satisfactorily explained by observing that mastering or introducing new words adds to the stock of concepts at a person's disposal – and on the face of it learning new words requires deploying old concepts. But if distinctions of meaning turn out to depend upon prior conceptual distinctions, then it is no argument for the claim that thought requires language to urge that the content of the former can be explained only in terms of the latter.

It might be objected that we have overlooked this point: that grasp of the meaning of a word can be explained in terms of something other than possession of an associated concept. If this were so, then the following argument would take shape: what it is to possess a refined concept cannot be separated from understanding an appropriate word, and this latter is a matter of employing the word in a certain way; so we can explain what possessing a concept is in terms of *using* a word; and this means that there is no circularity in the argument that content differences among thoughts depend upon differences of meaning. This argument improves on the one that preceded it, but it shares with it a premise we should find dubious: this is the idea that, at least for some concepts, the *only* way in which they can be manifested is in the use of words, and so their possession can only consist in propensities to linguistic behaviour. But it is by no means obvious that this premise is correct; indeed there is considerable plausibility in the principle that for any concept there is *some* conceivable way of manifesting it which is not linguistic in character. This should be clear for simple concepts of observable qualities – for example, colour concepts – since sorting behaviour would show a distinction. But even for complex concepts it always seems possible to think of *some* sort of behaviour which would manifest (albeit non-conclusively) their possession: consider the concepts of *water, monarch, motor car, death, desire,* and so forth. If this principle is correct, then no concept is essentially such that it is manifestable *only* in speech; and so we still have no argument yet for the thesis that some concepts cannot be possessed by creatures without language. If there is a sound intuition that sophisticated concepts require language, we have yet to expose its source. We shall mention two more attempts to do this.

We are familiar with the fact that a novel notation may facilitate thought, either because of its greater perspicuity or by dint of economy. The ability of symbols to make thinking more efficient may suggest an explanation of why the exercise of complex concepts requires language: words can become associated with complex concepts and, in so doing, stand in for those concepts in thought – words thus stand proxy for concepts. The idea here is that naked concepts are apt to be cognitively unwieldy; employing a symbol for a concept can effect savings in cognitive space. No doubt, it will be admitted, this process is something of a mystery, psychologically, but still it does go on: words function as a code for concepts, and like codes in general they abbreviate and simplify. The objection to this suggestion is not that words do not function in this way, nor that their doing so is puzzling (though it is) – the objection is rather that this is not the right *sort* of justification for the thesis that there cannot be thought without language. For the suggestion relies upon a certain kind of cognitive limitation on the part of human beings and other animals, to the effect that they must compensate for their limited information-processing capacities by employing codes. But this seems just a contingent fact about the sort of thinker we are, of the same order as our incapacity to count in binary notation; it is not a consideration that will apply to any conceivable thinker, because we can imagine thinkers with greater cognitive capacities than ours. In short, if concepts require words merely as abbreviatory devices, then this requirement is not a conceptual one, since the need for abbreviation is just a contingent fact about the human and (terrestrial) animal mind. What is also left open by this suggestion is the possibility that concepts themselves might abbreviate other concepts, without the intermediary of words.

The second and final suggestion is the most radical of all: it tries to link the possession of concepts with membership in a society of communicators. As a matter of empirical fact it seems that we acquire concepts (in large part) by way of interaction with others; they correct our use of words and so instil the corresponding concepts in us. The radical suggestion is that all concepts are social in origin: to have a concept is to conform yourself to the practices of a community, and to acquire a concept is to become apprised of those practices. This is because, according to this suggestion, employing a concept is following a rule, and rules are defined socially – in particular, the idea of a mistake in the application of a concept can only be understood by reference to some community. Properly to assess this view of concepts would require detailed discussion of whether a creature can possess genuine concepts in isolation from any community, and whether sense can be made of a creature's possessing a determinate concept independently of the practices of others; but we do not need to undertake such a discussion, because even if the thesis of the social character of concepts were correct it would not immediately show that concepts require language. It would not show this, because some additional argument is needed for the claim that the relevant notion of a social community is that of a *linguistic* community: the conclusion of the argument is only that for an individual to possess a concept it is necessary that he interact with members of a community who correct his applications of the concept and who exemplify a common practice in respect of the concept; nothing has been said to demonstrate that such interaction and such a common practice must be linguistic in nature – interaction and practice might take the form of non-linguistic behaviour. The interaction might consist in certain kinds of reward and punishment, and agreement might consist in sharing your dispositions to sort things with the like dispositions of the community. So again we have no argument for denying thought to the speechless.

We have been unable to find a cogent argument for the thesis that thought is possible only in the presence of language. It would be rash to conclude positively that thought is conceptually independent of language, though the considerations we have adduced do *seem* to encourage that conclusion. And if thought can occur without speech, then the inner saying theory looks compromised – thinking is not, constitutively, done in words. What is the medium of thought, then? The obvious answer is that the constituents of thoughts are concepts; concepts are to judgements what words are to sentences. But of course to say this is not to say very much, for the real question is what a concept is; so the observation that we think in concepts is not a theoretical alternative to the thesis that we think in words – it is what the latter thesis purports to be a theory of. It would not be wrong to say that a concept is a 'mental capacity' – a capacity to behave, linguistically and non-linguistically, in certain ways. But this cannot be a finally satisfactory account of concepts, because we want to know in virtue of *what* someone has such a capacity. Unless we are to fall into a kind of behaviourism which tries to reduce concept-possession to behavioural dispositions, we need to be told what sort of intrinsic state of a person constitutes having a concept. Such a state will, presumably, be some sort of internal representation – though, again, this is to say little. A theory of concepts is a theory of what confers the mental capacities in the manifestation of which concepts are exercised. The old, and discredited, theory that concepts are mental images was, in spite of its failings, at least an attempt to answer this question. The hypothesis of the language of thought is in the same business, substituting words for images as the basis of the mental capacities conferred. The trouble with this theory of concepts is, fundamentally, that it is either inadequate or circular: it is inadequate if it tries to generate concepts from mere uninterpreted syntax; but it is circular once it concedes that the inner words need an interpretation, since this is precisely for them to express concepts – and it will be those concepts that are doing the work the inner saying theory arrogates to itself. To this fundamental question – What is a concept? – we have given no positive answer. But perhaps there is a way in which it is right to decline answering that question; for why should we expect there to be any *one* answer to the question what a concept is? Judgements and the concepts that make them up are very various, as various as the kinds of sentences and words there are; so perhaps we will not be able to provide any single answer to the question what a concept is – it will depend on the concept. This is not to say that nothing systematic can be said about concepts, but it should affect our view of what *sort* of systematic theory might be feasible. We can produce systematic theories of meaning, though we have become aware of the pitfalls attending the question 'What is the meaning of a word?' Words have it in common that they contribute toward the meaning of sentences, but little else can be said to unify them; in the same way it may be that concepts share no significant features beyond the fact that they contribute to the content of thoughts. But this reflection should not make us complacent in failure; for it remains true that we are hard put to it to come up with a satisfactory account of what any *one* concept consists in. The difficulty of providing such an account should make us tolerant of any suggestions that might come along.

5 Action

So far we have been chiefly concerned with cognitive mental phenomena – perceiving, thinking, introspecting and so forth. It is characteristic of cognitive states to represent the world as being a certain way, and such a state can be judged correct or incorrect according to whether the world is the way it is represented to be; the role of the cognitive is to *fit* the world. In the present chapter we turn to a range of mental phenomena whose role in the mind is of a different order: these mental phenomena belong to the *willing* side of the mind. The role of the will is not to understand the world but to change it; not to represent the world as it is, but to make it conformable with what the agent *wants*. Because of this the will is by nature active; cognitive phenomena, since they must bend to the condition of the world, may be described as passive in relation to the world they represent. The will effects change by virtue of its embodiment: to bring about material changes the will must be linked with bodily actions capable of working those changes. The focus of our interest will thus be upon the nature of bodily actions like raising your arm, hitting a drum, writing a letter. The will, we might say, finds its most natural expression in the performance of such bodily actions. Phenomena of will thus constitute one side of a fundamental division in the mind, at least as significant as the side comprising the phenomena of understanding we have dwelt upon so far. Before we investigate the active, practical side of the mind we must ask a question of a (by now) familiar kind: granted that the faculties of understanding and willing are found together in human beings and other animals, is this joint exemplification somehow conceptually necessary or is it a philosophically uninteresting fact of natural history? *Must* any creature that knows act, and vice versa?

One thing is clear at once: the knowing and willing halves of a mind do not operate independently of each other. What a creature knows informs its dispositions to act, and what a creature does affects what it knows. Thus perceiving a predator will prompt the will of an agent, and the resulting actions (fleeing etc.) will change what is perceived, which in turn will lead to appropriate action. There is evidently an interplay between the two halves of a mind; and this for a good reason.

Evolved creatures are intent upon preserving their lives, and bodily action is (for many of them) essential to their survival; but actions need to be guided by information about the world if they are to serve the end of survival. From this point of view action would be useless without knowledge, and knowledge would be pointless without action. Indeed, it begins to seem that the active side of a creature's mind is primary, since it is the *function* of perception and knowledge to guide and control action: cognitive phenomena can be properly understood only in the light of their role in informing action – creatures can think only because they must act. These considerations certainly demonstrate a tight bond between knowledge and action – it is entirely intelligible that we should find them exemplified together – but is the bond tight enough to qualify as *conceptual*? It is true enough that, given the conditions of animal survival we actually find, action that is uninformed about the external world will be apt to go wrong, and so it is hard to make evolutionary sense of the development of a faculty of knowledge about the external world that did not feed into action: but can we not imagine circumstances in which the exigencies of survival are very different and creatures came to exist otherwise than through the forces of natural selection? Suppose God decided to create some purely contemplative creatures, perceiving and knowing but not endowed with the will to move their bodies; or suppose He created a world in which acting to satisfy your desires did not require knowledge of the world – you just crook a finger to get what you want. Would any conceptual obstacle stand in the way of His implementing these decisions? It does seem clear that God *could* thus separate the faculties of knowledge and will as we actually find such capacities; these created creatures would not have their minds divided as we evolved creatures have ours. But it is less clear that He could shrink one of these halves to nothing while keeping the other: that is, it is unclear that we can make sense of a thinking mind in which *all* trace of the will has been obliterated, or a willing mind in which not a tincture of perception or thought is present. For, to realise the former possibility we would need to eliminate even purely mental acts such as concentrating the attention on something perceptually given or initiating a train of reasoning: since these are things we decide actively to do, God would need to create a mind in which neither is possible – but then it becomes less than obvious that we would still have perception and thought. Also such a creature would have to be embodied in some way, but then would it not have the capacity of at least *attempting* to act? In some way, then, it seems that a knowing mind must be an active mind, in which case there is a limit on the extent to which cognition can exist apart from conation. The existence of a limit is even clearer in respect of the converse possibility: although perception of the external world might not be necessary to bodily action, other sorts of cognitive state are not so easily eliminated – notably, awareness of the body and knowledge of one's own acts of will and their consequences for one's wants. It is very doubtful that we can make sense of an ability to act in the absence of these sorts of cognition. But note that such limits on the separability of cognition and conation do not stem from the evolutionary or life-preserving considerations we started with; these limits hold in virtue of conceptual connections that are quite independent of the fact that terrestrial animals are built to survive in a hostile environment. And the considerations that seem to require the joint exemplification of knowledge and will do not incline us to hold that the capacity to act is conceptually more basic than the capacity to represent the world. The conclusion indicated, then, seems to be that the two halves of mind are not accidentally joined, but that each half can be coherently conceived to be considerably truncated relative to what is empirically the case. And it is also true that *if* a creature has both faculties, in the way we do, then these faculties will be intimately connected in their operations.

Philosophers have been prone to take one or other of the cognitive and conative aspects of mind as fundamental, downgrading the importance of the less fundamental side; and this has enabled them *either* to claim that the mind (by which they typically meant the human mind) is essentially passive and contemplative, its office being to reflect the world; *or* to claim that it is essentially practical, its office being to treat the world as a repository of human instruments. Which of these emphases you choose will, clearly, shape your conception of the basic relationship between the mind and the world – and so will determine your view of how the mind conceives the world. Earlier centuries saw a greater emphasis on the contemplative and cognitive, with the mind passively bearing the imprint of the world; latterly the emphasis has tended to shift to the active and practical, with the result that our conception of the world has been supposed by some to be relative in some way to the ends that motivate our interactions with it. In so far as these contrasting emphases are prompted by the desire for a monolithic picture of the mind, they are surely misguided: the mind has both cognitive and conative faculties, and these faculties establish two sorts of relationship with the world which cannot be reasonably assimilated one to the other. The world is, on the one hand, the object of our practical concerns and is accordingly viewed as instrumental in relation to our wants; but it is also the object of disinterested representation, demanding to be depicted as it is in itself, independently of human ends. The world is that on to which our actions are directed, but it is also the object of contemplative thought. We are well advised, therefore, to look with suspicion upon philosophical systems that emphasise one side of the mind at the expense of the other.

But let us leave these big issues and address ourselves to this more tractable question: What is the difference between a bodily movement that ranks as an action and a bodily movement that does not? Take, as an example, raising your arm to wave to someone and your arm rising because of a muscle spasm. The intuitive distinction here is between a bodily movement in which the agent is active and one in which he is passive; but this observation by itself does not really advance us much beyond recording that the former is an action and the latter is not. How then should we explain the active/passive distinction? It is important, in developing an account of this, to recognise how simple and primordial the notion of action is. We miss this primitiveness if we concentrate on the actions of human beings endowed with reason: we will be tempted to think of actions as essentially the outcome of deliberative practical reasoning, backed with a full-blown intention. But it seems implausible to restrict the distinction between active and passive – between what a creature does or initiates and what merely happens to it – to agents thus intellectually equipped. For we want to apply the distinction to other animals to which we would be reluctant to attribute the power of practical reason: thus consider the difference between a frog flicking out its tongue to catch a fly and the same frog being knocked over by a gust of wind. And then there are (human) babies: before they attain the ability to reason and intend they are surely such as to invite the distinction between active and passive movements. Furthermore, there are movements of adults that are scarcely intentional and reason-manifesting, like twiddling the fingers or tapping the feet, that nevertheless count as actions. We might try to accommodate these last actions by claiming that they are degenerate cases of rational actions done with an intention; and this claim might be backed up with the suggestion that these are essentially conceived as the pointless actions of an agent whose actions are *typically* intentional and rational – they come from the periphery of a capacity at whose centre are acts of reasoned intention. But the actions performed by creatures lacking such a capacity cannot be similarly brought within the intellectualist theory; it is not really plausible to think of them as rating as actions only because they are the first step on the road that leads to rational intentional action. In order to encompass both the primitive and the sophisticated forms of action, then, we need a more abstract conception of the active/passive distinction which the two forms can be seen as specialising. A natural suggestion is that actions are bodily events which are teleological: they are movements directed toward some future state of affairs in which the agent's needs or desires are satisfied as a result of the action. This more general notion of purpose enables us to include the frog's tongue-flicking as an action, as well as a human being's signing of a peace treaty, since both have their purpose – to obtain food and to get re-elected, let us say. On this broad conception of action the notion is not a sharp one: it shades off into events that hardly count as actions, such as the light-sensitive behaviour of plants, and it admits of borderline cases. This seems right, though, because the active/passive distinction has very general applicability, even when restricted to active events serving a purpose. The basic notion of action is the idea of a movement whose causal source comes from within the agent and which occurs because of some purpose the agent has. When we try to make the notion more precise or restricted we find that we are arbitrarily excluding certain cases or stipulating a more refined notion.

Rather than trying to excogitate interesting results by concentrating on the very elastic concept of action, let us turn to the notion of will; and let us make the object of our concern the idea of a willed movement. The idea of a willed movement is narrower than the idea of an action done for a purpose; it corresponds more closely with what philosophers have wished to circumscribe in talking of action. Peristalsis is an action of the body which serves a purpose, but it is not a willed movement; and the goal-directed movements of very lowly animals may be styled actions even though they are not manifestations of will. The idea of a willed movement stands somewhere between the broad notion of action and the restricted notion of actions done from reason. At one extreme we have the movements of psychologically primitive organisms such as insects, which invite the action/non-action distinction; at the other we have the deliberative actions of human beings. We do not want to credit insects with will, but neither would it be right to limit will to the intellectually endowed. A test of whether the concept of will applies to a creature is whether it is correct to speak of it (non-metaphorically) as *trying* to do something: we do not speak literally of worms trying to get to the damp, though getting to the damp is (at least sometimes) something they *do*, not something that merely befalls them; but we are ready to allow that a cat is trying to catch a bird or that a monkey is trying to reach a banana. In these latter cases we need not also be prepared to say that the creatures concerned have formed corresponding intentions, still less that their actions are the outcome of reasoning. Applying the concept of trying, and so the concept of will, seems to require that the creature have psychological states, specifically needs and wants, but it does not call for the full panoply of practical reasoning. The concept of will is thus more primitive than the concept of reason, but it is less primitive than the ordinary broad concept of action. Our central topic, then, is best described as that of willed movement; but let us, from now on, call this type of event *action*, explicitly acknowledging this to be a stipulated philosophical usage: this will be less cumbrous and also bring our terminology into conformity with the usage that has become standard in discussions of the topic of willed movement.

The way in which we have distinguished our topic already gives a clue to the nature of action: an action is something which has two aspects or 'moments' – one corresponding to the idea of will, the other coming under the idea of movement. Raising your arm somehow incorporates both willing to raise your arm and your arm rising. This seems intuitively right: from the agent's point of view raising his arm involves some sort of psychological event, which we are calling an event of willing; but also, as is evident by taking up the third-person perspective, raising your arm involves a bodily movement, the arm going up. Actions, then, are psychophysical entities; they have an inner and an outer aspect. This is shown in the fact that we do not allow that an act of arm-raising has occurred unless *both* the agent has participated in an internal psychological occurrence – a willing – *and* his body has moved in the appropriate way – his arm duly rose. We must now enquire exactly how we are to incorporate these two aspects into the concept of an action.

We said just now that trying was a mark of willing: creatures can will if and only if they can try. But is all willing trying? If exercises of will were always and necessarily instances of trying, then we could say that all actions, in our stipulated sense, involve trying; and this would be to explain the philosophical concept of will in more everyday terms – in psychological terms we regularly employ. Trying is inherently active, and it would serve as the psychological aspect of action. We do not, of course, always *say* of someone who acts that he tried to do that which he did – for that might suggest that he experienced some difficulty in doing the action. But this does not imply that it is *false* to claim that agents try to perform even their most effortless actions. We should divide the question into two parts: instrumental actions in the performance of which you do one thing *by* doing another – for example, directing the traffic by raising your arm; and non-instrumental or basic actions in which the action is not done by doing something *else* – for example, simply raising your arm. It would, in the ordinary course of things, be odd and misleading to say, in respect of the first sort of case, that the policeman directing the traffic was trying to do so, if he was succeeding perfectly well; but imagine that, unknown to him, the traffic was not proceeding as he intended – it would then be in order for him to say, perhaps in self-exculpation, that he was trying to direct the traffic. Similarly, there seems no difference, with respect to what is going on in you psychologically, between the normal case in which your arm rises as a result of your decision to raise it and the abnormal case in which, unknown to you, your arm has been paralysed; yet in the latter case we would say that you did at least try to raise your arm – and your mental acts were no different in the former case. You say that you tried to do something when you doubt that you have managed it; but if you did in fact manage it this does not cancel out the ascription of trying. Since any bodily action is subject to such doubts, we can always imagine external conditions making it appropriate to say the agent tried; but these do not affect the nature of the inner psychological event that goes towards the action – so we can legitimately claim that there is always an event of trying involved in any action. With this shown (or at least made plausible) we can now ask what the relation is between the trying and the action, and so give an account of what sort of thing an action is. We shall consider four theories, rejecting all but the last.

The first theory accepts (as do the others) that an action is a willed movement, but it identifies the action with the movement alone, holding that the movement counts as an action in virtue of its antece-dents, among which the trying is included. Thus the action of arm raising is identical with the movement of arm rising; the trying is thus not in any way *part* of the action, since it is clearly not part of the arm rising. This theory may be compared with an analogous (and pretty obviously correct) theory of what makes an experience perceptual: it is not anything intrinsic to the experience that makes it perceptual but is a matter of an extrinsic relation, causal in nature, to the object of the experience. Similarly, according to the first theory, actions do not differ intrinsically from mere movements: the two are distinguished by the presence or absence of a relation, possibly causal, to some extrinsic item, namely a trying. Just as the veridicality of an experience is not something you can read off from an intrinsic description of the experience, so the status of a movement as an action is not something contained in the movement itself: movement is to action as experience is to perception. The trouble with this theory of action is that it does not make the activity of the action constitutive of its being the action it is: since the movement can be conceived without the prior trying, we have to say that the action can exist as a non-action – actions are contingently actions as perceptual experiences are contingently perceptual. But this seems very implausible. Suppose we take a segment of an agent's biography ascribing a series of actions to the agent: then on the first theory the same actions would have been performed if we delete the fact that the corresponding movements issued from exercises of will – if, that is, the agent were related to his movements as a mere passive observer. But in these circumstances it would be wrong to say that the agent *did* anything, and so wrong to say that the action-ascriptions in the original biography are still true. Actions are necessarily things you do, but mere movements, considered separately from events of willing, are not done at all. So the first theory, by identifying actions with movements, fails to register the essential activity of actions. We evidently need to bring the inner trying into more intimate relation with the action.

The second theory aims to meet this desideratum by going to the opposite extreme: it identifies the action, not with its outer aspect, but with the inner aspect – actions are identical with inner tryings. On this theory, then, raising your arm is identical with trying to raise your arm, where the trying is a wholly mental event. Just as raising your arm comes to be an action of directing the traffic in virtue of its consequences, so – on this second theory – trying to raise your arm becomes raising it in virtue of its consequences. This theory makes the bodily expression of the will a contingent extrinsic matter, not different in kind from the effects in the extra-bodily world that our actions may bring about. This theory also seems very implausible. Suppose you perform a series of actions with certain consequences beyond the body. We can readily imagine that these consequences did not obtain, and our doing so does not incline us to say that in these circumstances no actions were performed, though in the imagined case they had no extra-bodily consequences. But if we imagine further that no bodily movements occurred, perhaps because of paralysis, we should be inclined to say that *no* actions were performed. To put it differently, we can say of an action of directing the traffic that *it* could have occurred without being describable as directing traffic, since we can shear off the consequences of the basic act of arm-raising; but we cannot plausibly say, of an act of arm-raising, that *it* could occur and not be describable as such – the arm-*rising* cannot be sheared off. Actions like raising your arm are essentially movement-involving: to act thus is to move your body, the consequences being as may be. This is shown in the point that we can *see* someone's actions when we see him move his body; but on the second theory all you see are the consequences of the agent's actions, never the actions themselves, since the tryings with which actions are identified are purely inner events, invisible to the naked eye. The basic mistake of this second theory is to treat the relation between body and will as the same in kind as the relation between will and external objects; an adequate account of action needs to bring movements of the body and actions into more intimate relation than this theory does. An action is no more the cause of a movement than it is the effect of a trying.

The third theory acknowledges the need to make trying and movement constitutive of the action: it proposes to identify action with *successful* trying; the trying does not cause the movement – it encompasses it. In taking an externalist view of trying, this third theory construes trying as a kind of mental event which (when successful) reaches out to the body: it is an event which originates in the inner recesses of the mind or brain and has its culminating end-point in the movement of the body. This theory has the great merit of attempting to do full justice to the idea of an action as a psychophysical entity, by conceiving trying as itself incorporating a physical component, the movement. However, the third theory faces a forceful objection, namely that it does not seem true that tryings are intrinsically psycho-*physical*, even when they are successful. Suppose you try to raise your arm and succeed – your arm rises: surely we can imagine that very event of trying not being successful, because of paralysis. So the trying could occur without the movement; but in those circumstances the action would not have occurred. In short, tryings are contingently successful, but actions are necessarily successful, in the sense that they comprise movements essentially: actions *necessarily* have an outer aspect, as the third theory acknowledges, but tryings do not, as the third theory fails to notice. So this theory does not incorporate movement into action in the right way.

The fourth theory results from a small modification of the third: it gets trying directly into the act, but also includes the movement, while recognising that the trying ends before the movement begins. The picture is this: the trying occurs, closely followed by the movement, these being related (let us say) as cause and effect; the action is then identified by the fourth theory with trying and movement *taken together*. More precisely, the action is held to be *composed* of both the trying and the movement – or equivalently, is said to be identical with a complex event having these as constituents. Since the action has these two items as constituent components, it is neither caused by the trying nor the cause of the movement – for causal relations do not hold between events and their constituents. Moreover, the action is *essen-*

tially both a trying and a movement, since the aggregate of these two has them essentially as components. What the theory does imply – and this may seem at first sight a surprising result – is that concepts like that of *arm-raising* apply to entities that are conceptually and ontologically hybrid – being made up of a mental and a bodily part. Any expectations of ontological simplicity in the notion of action are therefore disappointed by the fourth theory. But such expectations probably have a suspect basis, traceable to the tension between first- and third-person perspectives on action. When we think about action from the point of view of the agent we concentrate on the inner events of will, and these are not themselves hybrid; when we take up the observer's point of view we think of actions as bodily movements, and these again are not hybrid. From each perspective, then, the concept of action seems unitary; going from one to the other we confusedly feel that one or other must afford a unitary account of what an action is. But once we recognise that both perspectives need to be brought into systematic co-ordinatioin, neither of them dominating the other, we will find ourselves prepared to accept a non-unitary account: since the concept of action, more so than any other mental concept, requires to be viewed equally from both perspectives, we should not be so surprised that it turns out to have the duplex structure the fourth theory claims. We expect otherwise only because of the general difficulty of combining the two perspectives. The composite conception of action thus seems to meet our desideratum of displaying actions as inherently psycho-physical more successfully than the previous three suggestions. An action is a willed movement precisely in the sense that it is a willing combined with a movement.

We have been making heavy use of the notion of trying; it is time to examine the nature of this mental phenomenon more closely. We shall consider three questions: How does trying or willing fit into the taxonomy of mental phenomena with which we have been working hitherto? What sort of directedness, if any, does the will exemplify? How is trying related to other mental states and events implicated in the production of action?

In Chapter 1 we divided mental phenomena into sensations and propositional attitudes, each class with its distinctive characteristics: does trying fall into either of these classes? It does not seem like a kind of sensation, since it does not have the sort of phenomenology characteristic of sensations; and it is also, what sensations are not, essentially active in nature. It does not seem natural to speak of what it is *like* to act and hence to try: willing is impalpable in a way sensations are not. On the other hand, though, trying does share some of the characteristics of sensations. Trying is necessarily conscious and infallibly known: if you are willing a bodily movement this fact must be present to consciousness – we can make no sense of unconscious trying. This point is not undermined by the consideration that there are descriptions of what an agent is trying to do that the agent is unaware of – as when a psychoanalyst says that his patient, in losing a photograph of his father, was trying unconsciously to get rid of his father. In such a case we are describing the agent's trying in terms of his reasons, and *these* can be unconscious; the claim about the necessary consciousness of trying is rather that *basic* trying – trying to move one's body – has to be conscious. Non-basic trying, as in the psychoanalytic case, comes from combining a basic trying with a belief about the results of moving one's body: these beliefs may be unconscious, but the trying they combine with cannot be. A second point of resemblance to sensations is that, as remarked above, trying is a primitive and pre-rational type of mental phenomenon: a creature can try though it is bereft of the power of reason. In fact it seems that, at least for terrestrial animals, having sensations and performing willed movements go together, both preceding the dawn of rationality. These similarities with sensation make it implausible to claim that trying is a propositional attitude; and indeed grammar encourages this conclusion – we say that someone tries *to* raise his arm, not that he tries *that* his arm should rise. In view of these points we should, it seems, accord the phenomena of will a *sui generis* status in our mental inventory; the active side of the mind has a nature of its own.

Trying is like perception, and unlike bodily sensation, in being directed on to something beyond itself – it has something like representational content. The primary object of its directedness is the body, or rather those parts of the body over which the will has control: we specify what someone tries to do by describing the bodily movement he wants to bring about. Again, we need to invoke the distinction between basic and non-basic tryings; the latter do not add any *new* events of trying, but rather consist in describing the basic tryings in ways licensed by the agent's beliefs. We can then say that the body is the immediate object of the will. Just as you can see one thing by seeing another, so you can try to do one thing by trying to do another. The termini of these series are the immediate objects of perception and will; instrumental belief thus has the logical role in the case of willing that the part–whole relation has in the case of perception. Now what sorts of concept shall we use in specifying the content of a basic trying? It is clear that the descriptions of bodily movements that ascriptions of trying employ are entirely general – you try to perform *an* act of raising your arm – but this is for an uninteresting reason, namely that the movements do not exist to be referred to as particulars until the trying has been successfully carried out. Trying is directed to future movements; so it can be related to those future movements only by way of the satisfaction of the general concepts giving the content of the trying: if the trying succeeds a particular movement *fits* the content of the trying. But we can also ask, more interestingly, about the directedness of the will on to the bodily *parts* involved in future movements; for these exist at the time of the trying, in rather the way perceptual objects exist at the time of perceiving. We said in Chapter 3 that the content of perceptual experience is purely general: is this true also of the content of trying in respect of bodily parts? The question is admittedly a strange one, but not unaskable; and the answer seems to be that the content of trying *is* likewise general. Suppose we give a particular limb of an agent's body a name – say we call the agent's right arm 'Stanley'. Now when this agent tries to raise his right arm should we give the content of his trying by saying that he is trying to raise Stanley? Superficially this may seem acceptable, until we reflect that if we were to replace Stanley with another arm capable of all that Stanley is this would not alter the content of the agent's trying: his trying would stay the same in content though the particular limb it engaged with would be numerically different. In short, you do try to raise your arm, but its being *that* arm – a particular physical object outside the mind – is immaterial to what you try: you try, we might say, to raise *whichever* physical arm is appended to your will in the appropriate way. This is not to deny that your trying is directed at a particular limb; it is so directed, but only in the way that perceptual experiences are directed at particular external objects: there is a notion of content for both which is independent of the identity of these objects and even of their existence.

The directedness of trying is not plausibly viewed as a species of *acquaintance*. This is obvious for the events of movement, since these are in the future relative to the trying; but it is also true of the body itself. To direct your will on to a limb is not to direct a perceptual faculty on to it: though trying may be structurally analogous to perceiving, it is not a special case of perceptual acquaintance. It is, however, very intimately bound up with a certain kind of acquaintance, for you are acquainted with the body on to which your will is directed: that is, you do perceive, by proprioception and kinaesthesia, your limbs and their disposition, and your doing so is clearly somehow connected with your ability to move your limbs at will. This raises the following interesting and curiously perplexing question: is it possible to perform willed movements in the absence of such acquaintance with the body? There is no doubt that the special relation between the body and the will which makes us say that moving our body is all that we really do is somehow connected with the fact that we have a special awareness of the properties of that particular physical object which is our body: the body is the immediate object of the will precisely because we are thus aware of it from the inside. Can it be just an accident that basic trying is limited to bodily parts with which we are in this way acquainted? A superficial answer to this question is that bodily awareness is what enables us to monitor the progress of our actions – to do something successfully we need to be aware of what we are doing. This answer is superficial because we can imagine all manner of ways in which an agent might be provided with information about the progress of his movements which do not depend upon the sort of bodily awareness we all enjoy – he might, for example, simply be told of the condition of his body by a scientist who has occluded all bodily awareness by severing the proprioceptive nerves. Since this is so, the suggested answer does not demonstrate why action and inner bodily awareness must go together. Another answer is that it is just a fact of biology and empirical psychology that this sort of knowledge of one's movements is more efficient than any other, conducing better to the agent's survival. But there seems to be an intuition that suggests more than that: we might put it, metaphorically, as the thought that, without bodily awareness, an agent would not know where to point his will – he would be robbed of a target at which to aim. Imagine, if you can, being deprived of any inner awareness of your body: there is a blank where your 'body image' used to be. You are now asked to raise your arm. There is an intuition that you wouldn't be able to set about obeying this order, even if you were told just where your arm was. You might be able to try to do something which you think will bring about, instrumentally, the raising of your arm, but there seems something problematic about just directly carrying out the order. In fact, the case is not unlike the difficulty of trying non-instrumentally to move objects other than parts of your body: this seems impossible, not because your motor nerves are not properly fixed up to tables and chairs – we might imagine them so fixed – but rather because these are not parts of a body of which you are proprioceptively aware. If there is this conceptual difficulty in willing movements without a foundation of bodily acquaintance, then it is not possible to conceive of a creature with a will like ours but lacking our sort of bodily awareness. But the question is difficult and intuition falters – perhaps because it is so hard to carry out the requisite thought-experiments.

The third question we put concerned the relation between trying and other aspects of the practical capacity. We made trying a component of acting; we must now examine the antecedents of action. The question comes in two parts, according as the action in question is that of a rational creature or not. The minimal antecedents of willed movement seem to be a psychologically expressed condition of need and some state functioning as information about instrumental relationships: thus, for example, the frog has a need for food, and also some state or mechanism which connects getting food with flicking out the tongue at passing flies. Given these antecedent psychological conditions, the frog will act when the appropriate time comes. For creatures like us, the important antecedents are desire, belief and intention. Thus if someone desires to visit his neighbour and believes that knocking on the neighbour's door will facilitate a visit, and hence forms the intention to knock on the neighbour's door, he is thereby prepared to exercise his will – he then tries to knock on the door, and with luck succeeds in performing the intended action. The desire provides the point of the action, the belief specifies the means of arriving at the point, and the intention constitutes the resolve to do what is necessary to get to the point. Desire supplies the impelling force, belief converts this force into something practical, intention prepares the agent to undertake the indicated action, and will puts the whole plan into action. To know why an agent acted as he did we need to reconstruct these antecedents, showing how they fit together into an intelligible pattern.

It is worth pointing out that the constituent elements that make up this sequence of mental events and states cannot be explained in terms of other elements in the sequence; in particular, intention cannot be analysed in terms of desire and/or belief, and willing cannot be reduced to intending. It is obvious that intending to do something goes beyond having a reason to do it, since you do not always intend to do that which you have a reason to do – you would have far too many (and conflicting) intentions if this were so. Neither is intending the same as believing you will do the intended action, since you may believe this on grounds other than that of having the intention, and because it is possible to intend to bring off what you believe you will probably fail to bring off. Nor is intending the same as desiring to perform the action in question, even when the desire is (in some sense) your strongest desire, since you may desire to do a certain something more than any other thing and yet still not intend to do it because you know or believe it to be impossible of achievement – consider the yearning of some people to travel to the stars. Desire is unfettered by knowledge of what is practically possible, but intention needs to reckon with the practical facts of life, as these are seen by the agent. Intending is what channels desire and belief toward the will; forming an intention is like putting the active faculty into gear, without yet depressing the accelerator. But intending is not the *same* as willing, since willing is part of action while intending is preparatory and antecedent to it. Also you can intend to do what you do not, in the event, will to do: you may intend to put a question to the distinguished speaker, but lose your nerve (will) at the last minute, though the intention may survive. We can say, if we like, that to will something is for the state of intending to be 'activated'; but this does not really explain willing in terms of intention, because the notion of activation thus appealed to is a mere metaphorical surrogate for the notion of willing: for an intention to be activated is just for the agent to try to do what he intends – certainly we cannot reasonably compare this 'activation' of intention with (say) the activation of an explosive material by surrounding conditions. Without the will, then, intentions would never get off the ground. So the transition from reason (desire and belief) to intention and thence to trying is a transition to genuinely distinct mental states or events, progressively closer, temporally and conceptually, to bodily action.

Having sketchily anatomised the mental antecedents of action, we can now ask how these antecedents lead from one to the other: is it right to say that the sequence of mental states is held together by the relation of *causality* – so that reasons cause intentions which in turn cause tryings which in turn cause bodily movements? In asking this we need to separate out three distinct questions: First, is it in fact the case that our practical mental states are causally related? Second, is the existence of such causal relations conceptually contained in the notion of action? Third, when we cite such mental states in explaining someone's action are we engaging in causal explanation? The first of these three questions is not, in itself, of any special interest to us, since an affirmative answer to it does not entail an affirmative answer to the philosophically interesting second and third questions: it might be that conceivable creatures do not exhibit the causal connections we do yet still count as acting; and it might be that the explanatory force of these ascriptions does not derive from the causal relatedness of the ascribed states. But it is also the case that the second and third questions are logically independent: for it might be that rational explanation is causal even though the applicability of the concept of action does not require a causal condition; and it might be that the concept is causal but rational explanation does not rest upon this causal condition. The first possibility would be the analogue of the following position on perception: that facts about physical objects do causally explain our perceptual experiences, but it is logically possible to perceive things that do not causally produce the perceiver's experience. Similarly, it might be held that when we can explain actions in terms of mental states the explanation is causal, but that there are conceivable cases in which action occurs though no such explanation can be given. Conversely, it might be said that the concept of action does require a causal connection with antecedent mental states, but that the explanatory force of mental ascriptions is a matter of the justifying logical relations that hold between mental states and action. To answer the second question we need to scrutinise the concept of action; to answer the third we need to examine the concept of explanation. It is not that we shall conclude that the questions have different answers, but we cannot hope to deal with the questions properly if we are unclear what we are asking. And it is a notable fact that what are commonly called causal theories of action and perception are actually theories of different sorts of thing: causal theories of perception have taken it for granted that physical objects cause experiences and have focused on the question whether a causal condition is conceptually necessary for perception; whereas causal theories of action have tended to address the question whether reasons do or can cause actions and whether rational explanation is causal, and have hardly raised the conceptual question whether action, like perception, requires a causal condition. With the questions thus separated, let us begin with the second issue: can there be action without causation?

To ask this question is to ask whether a causal connection with prior mental states is *necessary* for action; later we shall go into the question of sufficiency. With respect to action the question has a complexity that does not attach to the analogous question about perception, since an action has two elements, trying and movement: we therefore need to ask whether the trying element has to be caused by antecedent states, and whether the bodily element has to be caused by the trying in order that it qualify as a constituent of an action. Now if a trying occurs and is suitably related to a movement, then we have an action, irrespective of how things stood with the antecedents of the trying; no break of causal connections with antecedents could prevent a trying being of the right status to compose part of an action – though it might perhaps count against the event of trying being a case of trying to do that which was intended or desired. So we can confine ourselves to the internal constitution of the action: is it then necessary, for a movement to be the outer part of an action, that the movement be caused by the trying? Let us consider the question on analogy with perception. We suppose that the movement matches the content of the trying; it is, for example, an arm-rising which fits the content of an instance of trying to raise an arm. Now the most challenging cases for a theory which requires a necessary causal condition of perception are cases of regular and designed common cause: we imagine that some super-scientist is causing a perceiver to have experiences of a certain character and *also* causing there to be objects around the perceiver fitting his experiences – all this, we can suppose, with total reliability. Do we think perception occurs under these imagined conditions? The intuitive answer seems to be (though there are those who disagree) that such a set-up would not be one in which anything was actually *seen*. We can now imagine an analogous set-up in respect of action: a super-scientist is causing an agent to try to perform various movements, say by interfering with his brain, and also causing his body to move in the attempted ways: but he blocks any causal connection between the trying and the movement, say by severing the motor nerves. Would we say that such a person raises his arm – that is, performs an *action* of that sort – when he tries to and the scientist causes his arm to rise? To make the question harder, suppose that the candidate agent knows that this is his situation, at least to the extent of knowing that his tryings are not causing his movements. Intuition wavers on the question whether he acts. Suppose you discovered tomorrow that this had always been your predicament and that it would continue to be so: would you think that, contrary to your earlier beliefs, you had never really performed an action at all and would never do so again – that you were, in this respect, like a paralysed man? There is some inclination to say that this would be the wrong reaction, especially once you became aware of the true cause of your movements. If this inclination is justified, then the trying and the movement need not be causally connected in order to add up to an action: you can raise your arm without the cause of its rising being your trying to raise it. Our inclination (such as it is) to allow this perhaps stems from the consideration that such movements would still serve their primary purpose, namely to effect such changes in the world as will lead to the satisfaction of the agent's desires. If the super-scientist produced a mismatch between movement and trying, so that the movement failed to fulfil its purpose, then we would be much less inclined to allow that actions occurred, even when there was a chance match.

However, there seems to be another consideration that inclines us in the opposite direction: this is the conviction that a movement can only go to form an action if the agent is *responsible* for its occurrence. That is, nothing can count as *my* action – the action I bring about – if its occurrence is due to some causal factor independent of my own causal powers. If my movements are caused by the super-scientist and owe nothing to my own will, then it does not seem that I can be said to *do* them – they are outside my control. The movements composing actions are events which fulfil the agent's purposes, but they are also events he has the power to influence: and in the imagined situation the first feature is preserved, but the second is lost. The first feature does not require a causal condition, but the second feature seems to call for precisely that. The difficulty of deciding the question turns upon which of these two features is the more critical to the concept of action – in particular, whether the second is absolutely constitutive of what it is to act. Probably the right conclusion is that removing a causal condition leaves something *like* action – quasi-action, we might say – but not quite the real thing. What also deserves note is that if causality is embedded in the concept of action, then it is so for reasons somewhat different from those that encourage a causal theory of perception; for there is no proper analogue of the idea of responsibility and ownership in the case of perception – we do not want to say that an experience which fails to be caused by an object does not *belong* to the object. The necessity for causation in the case of perception is plausibly connected with the role of perception in the production of knowledge about external objects; but this is not why causation is necessary to action.

Is a causal connection between trying and moving a *sufficient* condition for the movement to be part of an action and hence for an action to occur? When we discussed the analogous question about perception in Chapter 3 we raised the problem of non-standard causal connections: are there such problems in respect of action? We need a case in which a trying causes a movement which matches the trying, but the causation runs in such a way as to prevent us calling the composite of the two an action. Brief reflection reveals that such cases are easily devised. Suppose an agent has a paralysed right arm but does not know this; and suppose that the super-scientist has connected this agent's motor nerves to the arm of a corpse a hundred miles away in such a way that when the agent tries to move his arm a signal is transmitted to the corpse's arm which causes it to rise: in this case it seems wrong to suppose that any action has occurred. Or suppose that a paralysed man tries to raise his arm and by some extraordinary chance the corresponding brain event causes a freak chemical change which causes the muscles of his arm to contract otherwise than through the motor nerves – the blood in the arm is caused, we may suppose, to acquire an electric charge which affects the muscle: in this case it is true that the man's own arm rises as a causal upshot of his trying to raise it, but we would not say that he raised his arm, that is, performed that basic action. These examples show that it is not enough to bind willing and moving into action that the former cause the latter; some extra conditions are needed if we are to achieve a proper analysis, and there is no guarantee that the extra conditions will be causal in nature. Nor is there any reason to suppose – indeed our discussion of causality as a necessary condition gave us some reason to doubt – that the extra conditions will mirror the extra that is needed to yield sufficient conditions for perception. One point that is worth bearing in mind when comparing perception and action in this regard is that whether a movement ranks as part of an action seems to be very sensitive to how the agent views the movement – in particular, whether it features suitably in his practical plans; but nothing comparable holds of perception – it does not seem that a would-be perceiver can make his experience perceptual simply by *using* it in a certain way.

We must conclude, then, that the prospects for a causal analysis of action look somewhat dim: causation is perhaps a necessary condition, but it is hard to see how it could be rendered sufficient. This conclusion does not, however, settle the question of whether giving an agent's reasons for acting as he did is a species of causal explanation. To give an agent's reason for acting is to say why he willed the movement in question; so we can rephrase the question as that of whether specifying the agent's reasons for trying (and, on occasion, succeeding) is giving the causal history of the trying. It may seem to count against this thesis that the trying and its mental antecedents are logically related: given the agent's desires and beliefs, a trying with that content was rational. The case may be compared with explaining why someone *believes* a proposition by giving his reasons for believing it. If the agent's reasoning is deductive in character, then the sequence of mental states comprising the reasoning will exhibit logical relations; the train of reasoning will conform to certain normative principles of logic. The agent's reasoning, whether practical or theoretical, will not invariably be rational, but it will always be the *kind* of thing that may be logically evaluated. But no one would suggest that a sequence of logically related propositions, as displayed (say) in a logic text, are causally related; that would be to confuse logical consequence with causal consequence. The feeling then is that this non-causal relation of logical consequence somehow rubs off on the attitudes which take the logically related propositions as their objects. But in fact this feeling rests on a confusion between the propositions believed and the beliefs in those propositions: the former are indeed not causally related, but it does not follow that the belief states directed on to them do not cause other states and events. However, admitting a causal connection between such mental states is not yet to agree that rational explanation is causal, since what it is about a reason that explains a trying (or a belief) may not itself be a causally relevant feature. Nor is the case clinched by observing that we use the word 'because' when giving an agent's reasons for action – as when we say he raised his arm *because* he wanted to attract someone's attention – and noting that the same word is used in indisputable cases of causal explanation. This does not in itself prove the point because we often use the word 'because' in *non*-causal contexts (I just have): we say, for example, that a certain sentence is a theorem of logic *because* it follows from such and such axioms and rules of inference. So someone who wished to deny that rational explanation is causal explanation could claim that the 'because' we employ in that context is the 'because' of logical connection: to say the agent did something or believed something because he had certain reasons would be saying that those reasons *justify* what he did or believed, and perhaps that the agent appreciated this. And indeed, expecially if you consider the matter from the first-person perspective, this surely does correspond to at least part of the force of the use of 'because': when you say you did this because of that you are saying that the latter justified the former. Since part of explaining an action is showing why it was rational for the agent to perform it, and since this is a matter of logical relations between the propositional contents of the mental states implicated, it seems that rational explanation must invoke considerations beyond the holding of mere causal connections: for simply to give the mental cause of an action is not yet to suggest that the former is a good reason for the latter – we need to add that the propositions concerned are rationally related.

It should be emphasised that to claim that rational explanation goes beyond the mere identification of mental causes is not to deny that reasons cause actions – it is not even to deny that causation enters into their rational explanation; it is just to insist that this is not *all* there is to it. The best way to see this is to compare your use of 'because' when you think that your actions or beliefs are rational with your use of that word when you are citing a mental factor which you think does not justify what it is invoked to explain: in the former case you suggest that there is a logical relation between what is explained and what explains it; in the latter case there is no such suggestion. But it should also be stressed that rational explanation cannot do without a causal component, since we need a way of registering the fact that the cited reasons were *operative* in producing the action in question. Thus suppose an agent has two sets of reasons which both make rational (justify) a given type of action, and suppose the action is performed because of one set and not the other. Then it will not suffice as an explanation of the action to cite the agent's reasons and note their capacity to justify the action in question; we need also to specify which reasons were there and then operative – and this seems possible only if we invoke a causal connection. So rational explanation seems to combine two things: it identifies a reason of the agent's which displays the action as rational in virtue of logical relations; and it also asserts that this reason was in fact causally operative in leading to the action. If to claim that rational explanation is a species of causal explanation is to claim that it *includes* a causal component, then the claim is right; but if it is to claim that no type of explanatory factor is present in rational explanation which is absent in ordinary causal explanation, then the claim is dubious. Reasons are rational causes, but to say what it is about them that makes them rational is not the same as saying what it is that makes them causes. To put it differently: the normative considerations we necessarily bring to bear in rational psychological explanation do not derive from the causal character of relations among mental states; rational explanation involves us in acknowledging the remarkable propensity of the mind to subject itself to the dictates of logic, as well as to the promptings of causality.

In this chapter we have spoken freely of the agent – that which acts – but we have said virtually nothing of the nature of this entity. In earlier chapters we have invoked the idea of that which thinks and perceives and introspects, again without enquiring too closely what sort of thing it is that is the subject of these psychological states. It is now time to attempt some account of what it is that acts, thinks and perceives: in the next chapter, therefore, we address ourselves to the very important and very difficult topic of the *self*. When we have treated of this topic we will have filled in the blank in our earlier discussions of the various mental phenomena – the self being an essential constituent of those phenomena.

6 The self

The states and acts of mind are one thing; that which has them is – it would seem – quite another. We are concerned in this chapter to elucidate the nature of the *subject* of mental phenomena – the entity to which we ascribe sensations, perceptions, thoughts, desires, actions. The question as to the nature of the self is best put by asking 'What am I?'; the self is just what is referred to when the word 'I' is used. And it is significant that the question of the self is naturally formulated by using the first-person pronoun: it shows that the question lends itself to an approach from the first-person perspective – the question 'What am I?' is one that each person asks of *himself*. This is not to say that we cannot properly ask the question about other selves; but in doing so we mean to speak, in using 'you' or 'him', precisely of that which the other would speak of as 'I'. Nor is it to say that a third-person approach is quite inappropriate; here, as elsewhere, both perspectives need to be heeded and (if possible) integrated. But we shall see that the distinctive character of the question emerges most forcefully from the first-person perspective, when we ask about the nature of 'myself'. Our aim, then, is to discover what sort of thing it is that is referred to when one says 'I am in pain/thinking that it is Thursday/trying to raise my arm', as well as in 'I have blue eyes/weigh nine stones/was born in 1950.' Familiar as such reference to oneself is, we shall see that elucidating the nature of what is thus referred to presents considerable difficulties.

It is tempting, in the face of these difficulties, to suppose that the question of the self is a pseudo-problem, generated by a misunder-standing of the function of 'I'. That is, so the suggestion runs, we wrongly take 'I' to be a referring expression and then perplex ourselves trying to discover what kind of entity is thus referred to; but if we see that 'I' is not really referential in function, then we shall no longer be puzzled about the nature of the entity referred to – for there is none. That 'I' does not serve to identify a kind of object might be backed up with the claim that 'I' is strictly redundant, being used solely to draw the hearer's attention to the person who is speaking; or with the claim that 'I' has the sort of role 'it' has in 'It is raining' – not to indicate a kind of *thing* that is raining but as a kind of dummy grammatical subject. On the face of it these claims about the logical role of 'I' look implausible, but can we actually show them to be mistaken? Even if they were correct, they would not by themselves dispose of the problem of the self, though they would require us to find some other formulation of our question: we could always put the question by asking what personal proper names like 'Jack' refer to, and it would be mad to suggest that *these* picked out no kind of object; but the non-referential thesis about 'I' would spoil the first-person formulation of the question, and so rob the issue of its distinctive character. It is not enough, in refutation of that thesis, to point out that from 'I am thus-and-so' we can deduce 'Something is thus-and-so', where the 'something' asserts the existence of the entity 'I' referred to; for we seem equally entitled to infer 'Somewhere there is rain' from 'It is raining', yet it would be wrong to say that 'it' refers to that somewhere. So it could be countered that while it is true that, if 'I am thus-and-so' holds, then 'Something is thus-and-so' must also hold, the something in question need not be what is referred to by 'I'. We come nearer to a more probative objection by considering the systematic relations between 'I' and other indisputably referential expressions, such as other personal pronouns and proper names. If 'I am thus-and-so' is true, as uttered by John, then 'John is thus-and-so' is also true, as is 'He is thus-and-so' uttered by someone else in reference to John. It is hard to avoid the conclusion that the dependence of truth among these statements derives (in part) from the fact that 'I', 'John' and 'he' all have the same object as reference. The word 'I' seems to function in the way 'now' does in relation to 'then' and '11.20 a.m. 30 July 1981', namely to identify an entity to which various properties are ascribable. But even if 'I' were not in fact used referentially, surely we could stipulatively introduce a word to refer to what these other words refer to, this word to be employed only from the first-person perspective – and then we could formulate our question about the self by asking after the nature of the denotation of *that* word. Let us then persist in enquiring what sort of thing 'I' refers to.

This formulation does, however, suffer from a quite different defect: it limits the question to creatures equipped with language. In asking after the nature of the self of a creature by wondering what the creature refers to with 'I' we assume that the creature performs acts of reference; but it is very far from obvious that the question of the self arises only in respect of creatures capable of speech and conversant with the word 'I'. But we can easily remedy this defect by shifting to the level of self-directed *thought*: we then enquire into the nature of what is thought about when a creature has thoughts about itself. Such self-reflexive thoughts are what get expressed in utterances containing 'I'; so even when the first-person pronoun is in fact used by a creature, the real focus of our interest is in the subject of such self-reflexive thought. This way of posing the question of the self does, however, raise another potential objection, namely that we are now assuming that selves always have self-reflexive thoughts. If it were held that there could be a genuine self which had no such thoughts, then we obviously could not ask about its nature by wondering what sort of thing its self-reflexive thoughts were about. So are we requiring too much of a self when we presuppose that any self has the self-conscious-ness necessary to raise the question of the self about itself?

We can respond to this line of objection in one of two ways: we can either reformulate the question again, eliminating its first-person char-acter altogether by asking what sort of thing *we* refer to when we say (or think) of another 'He is thus-and-so'; or we can retain the first-person formulation and insist that the presupposition is correct. The former way is the easier, but it sacrifices something important in severing the question of the self from the first-person perspective. The latter way can seem dogmatically stipulative, but it grows on one. It seems merely stipulative because it is plausible to ascribe mental states to creatures lacking self-consciousness, and surely there must be a subject of those states – a thing which has them. Can we then reasona-bly maintain that there is something that has mental states only if what has them is *aware* of that something? This seems a fair point, but then isn't there also something implausible about supposing such simple creatures to harbour a *self*, a unitary centre of awareness? We can acknowledge both intuitions if we introduce a distinction between different kinds of psychological subject: there is the idea of a thing which exemplifies mental attributes but which does not *ipso facto* qualify as a self – this could be simply the animal in question, a certain kind of living body; and there is the idea of a psychological subject different in nature from the living animal body, and conferring upon a mind a kind of unity not conferred by the body. Then we can say that the mental states of simple creatures belong to subjects in the first sense, but the mental states of self-conscious creatures have subjects in the second sense. We could say that the latter sort of subject – the self proper – displays a special kind of unity: it has a unity which is properly grasped only from the inside. What this position implies is that the kind of unity a self exemplifies is bound up with self-consci-ousness; without self-consciousness the mind of a creature has no more unity than that conferred by its body – from the inside it is just a collection or succession of mental states. Self requires consciousness of self because the characteristic unity of the self cannot exist without the unifying and integrating power of self-awareness; so the self proper cannot be antecedent to consciousness of itself. If this is right, then we were not wrong to introduce the self as the subject of self-reflexive thought; indeed the naturalness of this approach testifies to the plausibility of the presupposition about self-consciousness upon which it depends.

Is possession of a self a matter of degree, a condition that admits of borderline cases in which it is indeterminate whether a self is to be ascribed to a creature? Some creatures clearly do not possess a self, though they have mental states; others definitely do – but are there intermediate cases? The question is hard to come to grips with, but it is plausible to suggest that the existence of the self is an all-or-nothing matter – you either have one or you don't. This seems to derive from the special kind of unity in a creature's mental life which the self confers: we feel, from the inside, that mental states either belong to a unitary thing or they do not – they could not fall between being unified and being fragmented. The unity of the self is the unity conferred by self-consciousness, and this unity cannot come in grades. So not only does the question of the self arise only when a creature has reflexive awareness; it also arises saltatorially.

The concept of the self is to be distinguished from the concept of a human being and from any other biologically based classification. Like other mental concepts, the concept of the self already contains the essence of what it specifies; but biological concepts do not do this – they wait upon empirical science to disclose what the designated biological kind consists in. As we might predict, then, the concept of self will cut across groupings of creatures made upon biological grounds, with the result that indefinitely many biological kinds may permit the ascription of selfhood to their members. An indication of this feature of the concept of self is this: if a creature understands the concept of self and this concept in fact applies to that creature, then the creature must know this – selves necessarily know that they are selves; but it is perfectly possible for a creature to grasp the biological concept of a human being and for this concept to apply to that creature, yet the creature not know that this concept applies to it – human beings do not necessarily know that they are human beings. The basis of an ascription of selfhood is manifest in the first-person awareness any person has of himself; but the basis of biological classifications is not in this way a matter of common first-person knowledge. Any account of the self must accommodate this feature of the concept.

These preliminary remarks have not been intended to rule out any of the classical theories of the self; we have sought only to identify the nature of our enquiry and allude to some of the considerations to which any satisfactory account must be sensitive. We shall now turn to an examination of the main doctrines regarding the nature of the self. These may be divided into three: theories which identify the self with the body; theories which explain the self in terms of various mental relations; and theories which take the concept of the self to be primitive and not to be explained in terms of anything else. The first theory tells us that 'I' refers to a (living) body endowed with mental attributes; the second theory says that the reference of 'I' is a complex entity constructed in certain ways from the mental states we take to belong to the self; the third theory claims that the self is a simple substance which is distinct from the body and is not reducible to the mental states of which it is the subject.

In order to assess these theories of the self we shall address ourselves to the question of 'personal identity'. As it is commonly understood, this is the question under what conditions a person may be said to exist over time: we judge that the person we see before us is the *same* person we saw last week, and the question is what such identity over time consists in for persons. Answering this question can be expected to shed light on the question what a self *is* – the primary focus of our interest – because it is reasonable to suppose that the conditions of a thing's identity over time depend upon what *sort* of thing it is: so if we know what kinds of change a self may sustain and still persist, we shall know what it is that constitutes a self – it will be that which cannot change without the self ceasing to exist. The method is to see what can be conceptually detached from a self and that self endure; this, it is hoped, will isolate the essential core of the person from the inessential accompaniments. But it should be remembered that broaching the question of personal identity is an indirect way of getting at our real interest. There is, indeed, a sense in which the question of the nature of the self must be conceptually anterior to the question of personal identity, since in order to determine what the identity of a person consists in we must bring to bear our concept of the person that is judged the same: the point of asking the question of identity is to help to lay bare the concept of self which is invoked to answer the identity question. Since the concept of the self determines the kinds of change a self may endure, we can hope to expose the concept to clearer view by consulting our intuitive judgements about the continued existence of a self under various sorts of real or imagined change. We might say that the issue of personal identity has a methodological, but not a conceptual, priority.

The problem of personal identity is often described as the search for 'criteria' of identity. Here we need to distinguish two ways in which the object of this search may be understood, and to note that the way that is relevant for us has an implication we do well to make explicit. The notion of criterion is ambiguous between the idea of a way *telling* that a certain sort of fact obtains, and the idea of what is *constitutive* of its obtaining: the former is an epistemological idea, the latter a metaphysical one. In application to personal identity, the distinction is between the *evidence* we use to judge of personal identity over time, and our conception of what this is evidence *for*. And there is no guarantee that what we actually use as evidential signs of personal identity will coincide with that which these are signs of. To take an extreme example in which these come apart: we can imagine a society in which judgements of personal identity were always made on the basis of documents the people carried around with them; these documents would be criteria in the epistemological sense, but they are obviously not criteria in the metaphysical sense – or else we would have to say that selves are constituted of documents! This is not, however, to say that the two questions are totally independent; they are dependent in the way that any questions are about what something is and how we tell what it is. But unless we are to assume that, in general, the constitution of reality and our methods of knowing about it coincide, we cannot take it for granted that how we judge of personal identitiy affords direct access to what personal identity consists in. In fact this danger of conflating the two senses of 'criteria' is somewhat reduced by the fact that philosophers typically allow themselves, in discussing personal identity, to consider imaginary or conceivable cases, without undue concern about their actual occurrence or practical possibility. This is just as well, for otherwise we run the risk of arriving at views of the self which are tainted with misplaced verificationism.

The question about personal identity is analogous to the question of the identity through time of material objects, where again we allow ourselves to consider merely conceivable circumstances with a view to teasing out what is constitutive of the enduring existence of a material object. But now that we are clear about what questions we are asking it becomes evident that this metaphysical question (though not the epistemological one) presupposes a *reductionist* view of the identity of the items in question. For we are, in effect, seeking an analysis of 'same person' (or 'same material object') which employs concepts of some other range: we are asking for an account of what personal persistence consists in which does not employ the concept of sameness of person. And this is to assume that personal identity is not a primitive fact. But this assumption should not be accepted uncritically, or else we shall not be open to the persuasions of the third theory we distinguished above: for the import of that theory is, precisely, that there *are* no (metaphysical) criteria of personal identity, since the notion of 'same person' is conceptually primitive. By contrast, the other two theories implicitly or explicitly accept the reductionist presupposition, thus taking it that identity of a self must be explicable in other terms. From this point of view, then, our inability to produce adequate criteria of personal identity (if we are so unable) would not necessarily reflect either our intellectual limitations or the recalcitrance of the topic or the incoherence of the notion at issue; it might just be a matter of the primitiveness and irreducibility of the concept of the self, and hence of the identity of the self over time. This is not, of course, to suggest that we should immediately embrace this irreducibility thesis and proceed to the next topic; but we should be open to the prospect of discovering that there is no analysis of personal identity such as philosophers have sought, on account of the conceptual primitiveness of idea of the self. This should emerge only as the outcome of a conceptual investigation, not be offered as a reason for refusing to undertake the investigation at all.

A heuristically good way to assess proposed criteria of personal identity is to employ the 'survival test': told of a certain kind of change under which the issue of personal persistence is moot, put to yourself the question 'If that happened to me, would I survive?' If your opinion is that you would survive the change contemplated, then the respect in which the change takes place cannot be regarded as a necessary condition of personal identity; but if your considered opinion is that undergoing such a change would put an end to you, then the respect in question is essential to personal identity. And similarly for whether some proposed condition is sufficient. In applying the survival test to some proposed criterion we must, it goes without saying, be sure that the account is not circular: if no criterion could pass the test without being circular, that would be tantamount to the irreducibility of 'same person'. With these preliminaries in mind, then, let us turn to the three theories we mentioned, beginning with the body theory.

The body theory is most favourably viewed as an account of personal identity which takes seriously the third-person perspective on persons; it starts from the thought that we identify other persons over time on the basis of bodily continuity. It also wishes to do full justice to the conviction that persons are essentially embodied beings: to be embodied, on this theory, is to *be* a body. The body theory thus conceives of each person as identifiable with a living organism, the criterion of identity for which is physical or biological continuity. What we have already said about the distinctive traits of the self may well make us undisposed to accept this pleasantly simple view; but there is also a very powerful criticism of it issuing from the survival test, to the effect that a person may have the same body as you but not be identical with you. Suppose your brain is surgically removed from your body and placed into a new body, perhaps exactly similar to your body, so that the resulting person has your brain in his skull: then it seems undeniable that in these circumstances you would survive and not the person who donated the body. It follows that it is neither necessary nor sufficient for your personal survival that your body continue to exist as the body of some person: not necessary because you could survive in someone else's body, by dint of brain transplant; and not sufficient because your body might be the body into which someone else's brain is placed. This possibility thus seems to refute the living organism view of personal identity, since it is a condition of sameness of organism or animal that there be bodily continuity. The reason for this is not, of course, that organ transplants *generally* determine personal identity, so that putting A's *heart* into the body of B likewise makes A continue to exist in the body of B; it is, rather, that there is something special about the *brain* which seems to carry the identity of the person in this case. What exactly this is is a matter of debate – to which we return – but it is surely part of the truth to say that the brain preserves a person's 'point of view' on himself and the world. Thus the brain transplant case is at its most compelling when you imagine yourself staying conscious throughout the operation, aware of your own continuing identity and of the fate of your body; imagining the operation being performed on someone else does not yield so unequivocal a verdict. None of this is to suggest that a person only contingently possesses a body, still less that persons are not necessarily enmattered: but it does show, persuasively enough, that the identity of a person is not to be explained as the identity of his body; the reference of 'I' does not shift as your brain assumes its position in a new body.

Such considerations, and the aforementioned mentality of the concept of a person, may well incline us to look with favour upon a psychological criterion. Personal identity, according to this second theory, is a matter of certain sorts of relations between mental states: we say that A is the same person as B if and only if the mental states of A bear these identity-conferring relations to the mental states of B. A criterion of this kind may be proposed both for identity across time and identity at a time: for the former, the relations in question will hold between mental states had at *different* times; for the latter, the relations will hold between mental states of A and B at a *given* time. A parallel type of criterion of identity may be given for material objects: objects x and y are said to be identical if and only if stages or states of x are appropriately related to stages or states of y. This general type of criterion of identity explains identity for a kind of object – persons or material objects – in terms of relations between items of some other kind which do not include the relation of identity. The question, then, is what relations will serve this purpose in the case of personal identity. We can quickly dismiss the suggestion that the relation of (exact) psychological *similarity* is what is wanted: this is not a necessary condition, since a single person may change psychologically over time (you may survive a religious conversion); and it is not sufficient, since numerically distinct persons may be psychologically similar. A more promising suggestion is that some kind of *causal* relation between successive mental states will furnish the materials from which personal identity is to be constructed. Memory will be one central example of such causal relatedness – earlier experiences cause later memories of those experiences; the retention (or revision) of traits of character will also depend (in part) upon causal connections with traits antecedently possessed; and the stream of consciousness itself depends (again in part) upon causal relations between successive mental events. Let us call this theory the 'mental connectedness' theory of personal identity. It is analogous to a causal theory of the persistence of material objects: temporally separated physical states are states of the same object if and only if they are causally connected in certain ways. The mental connectedness theory of personal identity is clearly a reductionist theory, inasmuch as it proposes to analyse the identity of persons in terms of other concepts, having to do with various mental states and their relations. To test whether this reduction of the self leaves out anything essential we need to ask three questions of it: Is such mental connectedness necessary to personal identity? Is it sufficient for personal identity? Can the theory be formulated without circularity?

To show that mental connectedness is not a necessary condition of personal identity we need a case in which there is survival without mental connectedness. The case of thoroughgoing amnesia suggests itself: we imagine a person all of whose memories, character traits and so on are extirpated, say by a super-scientist, and a new set of mental attributes introduced in their stead. In such a case the later mental states of the person would not be causally dependent upon the earlier mental states in the ways that are supposed to constitute personal identity. Would you survive such an operation? It is not self-evident that you would not. We need to distinguish two sorts of case here: the case in which totally dissimilar mental attributes are introduced after the amnesia, and the case in which they are precisely similar. Suppose that, as an example of the latter type of case, you are told that the extirpation of your mental states will take place in a split second and that a qualitatively identical set will be induced to replace the old ones, there being no causal connection between possession of the old set and possession of the new – you will blink your eyes and the operation will be over. It seems, in this case, quite implausible to claim that you do not survive, that such mental discontinuity is tantamount to death; but if you do survive, then mental connectedness is not a necessary condition of personal identity.

Now let us ask whether dissimilarity in the new set of mental states makes us say the person has ceased to be. Suppose that you are to stay conscious during the replacement of your mental states and thus be aware of the psychological changes to which you are subjected: you start with certain memories, character traits etc., and you end up with entirely different such mental states – but consciousness persists throughout. Would you survive? To answer this question it seems necessary to distinguish between the concept of the self and the concept of a person, concepts we have hitherto treated as interchangeable. There is a strong inclination to say that you would be a different *person* after the replacement, because sameness of person seems to require some degree of psychological similarity; radical changes of personality sometimes make us want to say that we no longer have the same person. But it does not follow that a new *self* – that is, a new subject of consciousness – would come to occupy your body when the replacement was complete. Indeed, it is natural (though logically dangerous) to say that you become a different person but remain the same self: the reference of 'I' stays the same throughout, though it is no longer correct to speak of the same person. This seems to be because the concept of sameness of person easily slides between a qualitative and a non-qualitative sense: sometimes it is taken to mean what we have meant by 'self' (the non-qualitative sense); sometimes it is taken to mean similarity of personality and the like (the qualitative sense). Thus in the above case we are inclined to think that we have the same person in the sense of same self, but we may also take sameness of person to connote similarity of personality etc. – and then we are inclined to judge that we have a different person. The ordinary notion of sameness of person thus seems to comprise *two* conditions: A is the same person as B if and only if (i) A is the same self or subject as B *and* (ii) A is sufficiently psychologically similar to B. In the case under consideration, it seems, the first of these two conditions is met, but the second is not – which is why we decline to judge outright that the person persists. In view of this complexity in the meaning of 'person', it is better for our purposes to employ the notion of the self; this notion corresponds more exactly to the subject of mental attributes – it does not include the attributes themselves in the way the notion of person does. So we can say that it is plausible that you – your *self* – would survive even in the first type of case; and this shows that causal connectedness and mental similarity taken together are not *necessary* to personal identity over time.

Is mental connectedness *sufficient* for personal identity? This question is hard to answer until we have rooted out possible circularities in the notion of connectedness: we cannot allow ourselves to employ a notion of mental connectedness which tacitly presupposes sameness of the selves between whose mental states the connectedness holds. Since it is perfectly possible for there to be relations of causal dependence between mental states of distinct persons – as when one person comes to have a belief as a result of what another says – we clearly need some restrictions on which causal relations between mental states are such as to link states of the *same* person. And it is in fact surprisingly difficult to supply any restrictions which do not import circularity and yet have a chance of working. (As we have seen in earlier chapters, causal theories can seldom deliver sufficiency.) A natural suggestion is that we appeal to the body or brain to limit mental connectedness to states of the same person in a non-circular way: we say that the identity-conferring causal relations between mental states must hold within the same body or brain. Our earlier discussion of the body criterion already rules out this restriction to the body, however, since mental connectedness between states of a single self can span numerically distinct bodies. Having recourse to the brain also raises a number of doubts: first, the mental connectedness theory comes close to turning into a brain criterion (to be discussed in its own right shortly) and to losing its purely psychological character; second, it is unclear what criterion of brain identity is being assumed – the danger being that circularity will threaten at a different point. Thus we can conceive of physically continuous brain matter subserving distinct selves, and the mental states of these distinct selves could have causal connections running across this brain – unless, circularly, we say that where there are two selves there we must count two brains; and we can also imagine a single self possessed of a brain with spatially separated parts – in which case either we concede that mental connectedness within a self can hold between distinct brains or we count the separated parts as a single brain precisely because they subserve a single self. In short, restricting the causal relations by recourse to such physical factors is either circular or insufficient. Our unallayed suspicion, then, is that the idea of mental connectedness needed to yield personal identity cannot be defined save by smuggling in the concept it is supposed to analyse.

But there is a further problem about sufficiency, which brings out something important about the concept of the self: this is that the persistence of the self presents itself as a further fact over and above facts about mental connectedness. It is hard to state this intuition in a way that properly differentiates it from a parallel claim about material objects; for anyone who suspects reductive accounts of the identity across time of material objects – that is, anyone who thinks that this is a primitive notion – will likewise hold that the persistence of a material object is a further fact over and above such facts as continuity in space and time and relations of causal connectedness. But it seems that the persistence of the self is a further fact in a deeper and more radical sense than that in which the persistence of material objects is. Suppose you are told that some future object will have the sorts of spatio-temporal and causal relations with the object in front of you that are characteristic of persisting objects: would you then believe that the holding of these relations left it an open question whether the future object will be identical with that present object? It seems that there is a sense in which such identity is supervenient on these sorts of relations: if two series of thus related stages are indistinguishable, and one series is underlain by a single enduring object, then it seems that the other series must be also. But in the case of the self such a supervenience thesis seems less compelling: it is more natural to want to say, when all the facts about causal and other relations between mental states have been specified, 'Yes, but will that person be *me*?' It seems easier to suppose that distinct selves underlie a given mentally connected series; it just is not enough for someone to *be* you that his mental states be related to yours in the ways the mental connectedness theory suggests. Thus it does not seem so inconceivable that two series of mental states should be qualitatively indistinguishable, one series constitute the states of a single self, and yet the other series not determine a single self but correspond to a succession of distinct selves. This intuition may or may not be ultimately defensible, but it is an intuition we seem to have. What the intuition suggests is that, according to the concept of a self that we operate, it is impossible in principle to construct a self from relations between mental states: something crucial is always omitted. A mental connectedness criterion will, therefore, never capture our notion of the self; and this failure seems of a different order from the alleged failure of analogous criteria of identity for material objects.

The case of the brain transplant operation might seem to invite the idea that sameness of self consists in sameness of brain, since the identity of the person seemed to follow the identity of the brain. We have already mentioned the problem of circularity that arises for this suggestion: we must avoid counting brains as the same only because they are associated with the same self. But there are other problems too. In the first place, it is hard to see how the concept of the brain could enter the analysis of the concept of a person, since our mastery of the latter concept does not depend upon our mastery of the former concept – you can know what a person is and never have heard of brains, let alone have any notion of their identity conditions. It therefore seems very implausible to suppose that our judgements about the identity of selves are based upon judgements of brain identity. This implausibility is shown in the point that there seems no necessity, of a conceptual kind, for selves to have brains of the kind we in fact have: our concept of the self would not be different if our brains had been made in other ways. Thus suppose the brain were replaced (like a child's teeth) at a certain time in a person's life: the old parts of the brain died away to be replaced by new ones, in such a way that it would be correct to say that a new brain was formed. This supposition would not entail that a new self came to be; we can imagine that suitable physiological processes preserved the self as the brain was replaced. In these circumstances, the same concept of self could be applied, associated with the same conditions of identity, though the brain and *its* identity conditions were different from what they actually are. Moreover, it is not obvious that the physical basis of a person should even fall into the category of substance; it seems conceivable that a creature's 'brain' should be of the nature of a *process*. The process would take place in a body enclosing physical organs that do fall into the category of substance, but we can imagine that mental events do not have a substance-like organ to call their own. Discovering this to be true of a creature's physiological make-up would not force us to revise our assumption that the self of such a creature was itself a persisting substance. Our conception of the individuality and persistence of a self is simply independent of the ontological status of the associated brain. Nor is brain identity sufficient to capture personal identity: the self ceases to exist at death, but the brain continues to exist; and the information that someone has your brain does not seem altogether to pre-empt the question 'Would that be *me*?' The self is the reference of 'I' and its defining features are those of the mental – in particular, the first-person perspective shapes our conception of the self; but the brain is a physical organ of the body, not different in kind from other physical organs, its nature a matter for biology and the other physical sciences. The brain is no more able to constitute the nature of the self than are the physical states of the brain capable of constituting the nature of the mental states of the self.

We have now reviewed the main theories of personal identity and found none of them to be satisfactory. The consequence of this is that the self is not to be explained in terms of any of the materials these theories invoke: the self is not the body, nor the brain, nor a construction from certain psychological relations. But should we find this so disturbing? Perhaps all it shows is that the concept of the self is a primitive concept – that the self is what it is and not some other thing. The only proposal that clearly meets the survival test is just that the future person be the *same person* as you; nothing else really adds up to this, and this can hold when all else is lacking. The question must then be what sort of thing it is whose identity over time is thus primitive; and the plausible answer is that the self is a simple substance whose essential nature can be captured only in non-reductive terms. But before we take this view of the self we must consider some challenging reasons for denying that personal survival is a matter of the identity of a simple substance over time.

It might well seem self-evident that the survival of a simple substance, such as we are prone to conceive the self to be, cannot consist in anything other than the circumstance that some future individual be straightforwardly *identical* with the self in question. But the following possibility has been supposed to cast doubt on this seemingly inviolable requirement. Suppose, as is medically possible, that the two hemispheres of your brain are surgically separated by cutting the nerve fibres which connect them; and suppose, as is at least conceivable, that the two hemispheres are removed from your skull and placed in new bodies to which they are appropriately affixed. Then, assuming that the hemispheres subserve the same psychological functions – as is actually only roughly the case, but imaginably precisely the case – it is evident that the result is two persons; two separate subjects of consciousness come to dwell in two bodies. We cannot say that either of the resulting persons is *identical* with the original, because they are not identical with each other and each has an equal claim to be identical with the original. So it seems that in such a case no future person is numerically the same as the person we started with. But now let us try the survival test: would you receive the news that you were to be the subject of such fission with the same dismay as that with which you

would view the prospect of total annihilation? Is brain division tantamount, in respect of survival, to brain destruction? If your answer to
this question is that fission is not as lamentable as death, then it
appears that there can be personal survival without continuing
personal identity. Fission cases thus appear to suggest that the self can
continue to be – can persist – by virtue of relations to future selves
which are not relations of identity. To be set beside such fission cases
are (putative) cases of fusion. Suppose one hemisphere of your brain is
detached and preserved while the other is destroyed; and suppose the
same thing is done to someone else's brain (to avoid complications we
can suppose the two persons to be psychologically similar); suppose
further that the two preserved hemispheres are hooked up to one
another in the usual way, so that a person results. We cannot *identify*
the resulting person with either of the originals, because they are
distinct from each other and each has an equal claim to identity with
the future person. But would you regard the prospect of such fusion
with another person as equivalent to death? If you do not take this
view, then again you seem to be allowing for survival without identity.

Cases of personal fission and fusion may be usefully compared with
the fission and fusion of entities of other kinds; and the correctness of
claiming survival in the personal cases defended by noting our readi-
ness to view these other cases in that way. Thus consider the kinds of
surgery to which plants may be subjected. First suppose (what may or
may not be botanically possible) that a plant is cut into two and the two
halves grown separately so as to produce two plants of the same kind as
the original. Again, the logic of identity prohibits us from describing
the relation between the original plant and the resulting plants as
identity; yet there is a good sense in which the original plant persists as
two plants – it is still 'around' in a way it would not be if it were simply
incinerated. Or suppose that two plants are halved and a pair of these
halves grafted together to give a new plant: there is no identity between
the fused plant and the plants it fused from, but it would not be wrong
to think that the originals have in some sense persisted. If we are now
asked to diagnose our intuition that plants can thus 'survive' fission
and fusion, the natural answer would be this: the *parts* of the original
plant still exist when they have been separated from other parts of the
plant; indeed it is true to say that there is a relation of *identity* here
between whole plants and parts of other plants. In a case of plant
fission, then, the content and force of the idea that the plant 'survives'
is that the future plants are *identical* with *parts* of the original; and
similarly, *mutatis mutandis*, for the fusion case. Looked at in this way
the claim of survival without identity seems reasonable enough: an

object survives if the whole of it survives, and it may also survive if its parts survive. The part–whole relation also seems crucial in the cases of brain surgery: your brain survives in a fission case because parts of it are identical with future brains, and in a fusion case the future brain has as its parts the (parts of) earlier brains. In just the sense in which plants can persist through separation and recombination of parts, the brain can do likewise.

This digression on the fission and fusion of plants and brains enables us to raise the following question: In agreeing that a *person* may survive in cases of fission and fusion are we tacitly conceiving the person strictly on the model of his brain – and if we are, is this legitimate? That is, are we regarding the self as subject to the same principles, with respect to the connection between survival and the part–whole relation, as these other non-personal entities? If we are, then we are presupposing a certain conception of the constitution of the self, and the question must arise whether this conception is really acceptable. It is important, in considering this question, to appreciate that the intuition of personal survival is not satisfactorily explained in terms of psychological similarity and causal connectedness: if this were the sort of fact upon which the claim of survival rested, then the claim would be vulnerable to the criticisms we made earlier of such accounts of personal *identity*. Short of a convincing defence of mental connectedness theories of the self, we cannot accept this account of what survival amounts to in the fission and fusion cases; indeed such an account of survival in the personal case is even less plausible than for the analogous fission and fusion cases involving material objects. The relation of being a *part* of an earlier object is a far stronger relation than that of having states which are causally connected with states of some earlier object. It seems, then, that the claim of survival in cases of personal fission and fusion must depend upon presuppositions concerning part and whole: the resulting persons in a fission case are being conceived as literally *parts* of the original, and a fused person is being taken to have earlier persons as parts. That is to say, we must be conceiving persons in the image of their brains when we agree that there is survival in these cases: we are supposing that selves may, quite literally, be divided into parts, as brains and plants may be so divided; and this is to suppose that selves *have* parts into which they can be divided. Now we have no difficulty in seeing that a divisible plant has plant-like parts; this we would assent to independently of the possibility of plant fission cases. But the suggestion that a self has self-like parts is not something we antecedently recognise as true, or even as immediately intelligible; this is something we are brought to believe only through reflection on fission and fusion cases. Ordinarily we regard the self as a simple and hence indivisible substance, not as a composite of selves or potential selves: our pre-theoretical notion of the self does not represent it as a compound or complex of self-like entities, in the way the brain is naturally conceived as a combination of brain-like entities. So if we are to go along with fission and fusion cases, and the thesis about survival they are invoked to demonstrate, it looks as if we must revise our ordinary conception of the constitution of the self; it is not the kind of being we had taken it to be.

This asymmetry with unproblematic cases of survival without identity should prompt us to review our initial intuitive reaction to putative cases of personal fission and fusion. Suppose we held, in obedience to our ordinary concept of the self, that the self is so constituted that it *could* not be literally divided: in being non-composite, it is not the sort of entity that can admit of detachment and separation of its parts. Then we should have to say that in so-called fission and fusion cases the resulting selves are *quite new* selves, not made up of the parts of old selves: when you split a person's brain you do not thereby split the person into two parts; rather, you create two totally new selves – and similarly when you fuse two brains (or brain parts) into a single self. This, at any rate, is the description of what is going on in these cases that would be preferred by someone wishing to cleave to the ordinary naïve conception of the constitution of the self. Does this description have any plausibility? Its plausibility cannot be appreciated by considering the matter from the third-person perspective; the image of the divided brain has too much sway from that perspective. But ask yourself whether you can really imagine, from the inside, having the centre of consciousness which is your self carved into two pieces, both of which *are* (parts of) the original self: to imagine this is to imagine that the point of view you now have should become two independent points of view both of which are still yours. But how can a single unitary point of view project itself into two such distinct and separate points of view? If (*per impossibile*) we apprehended ourselves as constitutionally composite, made up of sub-selves, this would presumably be no problem; but from our actual first-person perspective this seems an impossible way of understanding the sort of being a self is. These considerations, then, at least give some motivation for insisting that brain fission and fusion must be conceived to produce totally new selves. The important point is that the idea of a divisible self gains what coherence it has from the evident divisibility of the brain; without this the idea of personal fission and fusion would be reasonably dismissed as inconsistent with the simplicity of the self. The significance of this point about the role of the brain in these cases can be brought out as follows. Suppose we ask into how *many* selves a given self is divisible: if the self really has self-like parts, then we would expect that an examination of the self *qua* self should answer this question. But in fact the question and its answer cannot be intelligibly mooted without recourse to the nature of the brain associated with the self in question. Suppose that the brains of some persons have just one hemisphere capable of sustaining a self, that others have (like our brain) two, others twenty-seven, yet others a thousand: then the selves of each of these creatures will be said to have as many parts, and be capable of generating as many non-identical survivors, as the number of parts their brains have. This consequence seems extremely odd, since the selves of each type of creature will present themselves as possessed of the *same* unitary and non-composite inner constitution. (Contrast this with divisible plants of variously many parts.) Moreover, the trouble we have in projecting ourselves into the perspectives of two future selves seems compounded when the numbers increase; it begins to seem even more like making new selves out of bits of your old brain.

What we have here is a genuine collision between the way we antecedently conceive the self and the way fission and fusion cases invite us to think of our survival; no such collision attends the non-personal cases of survival without identity. This collision is what produces the peculiar unease and sense of being duped that we naturally feel when first confronted with alleged cases of personal fission; we obscurely feel that *something* is going wrong, though we are hard put to it to shape this unease into a principled resistance to the conclusion about survival we are asked to draw. This perplexity seems to issue from a prior commitment to the simplicity of the self which runs up against certain facts about the relation between the brain and the person. It is the strength of this commitment which motivates and explains why preserving *both* hemispheres of the brain might be reasonably viewed as less like survival than preserving just one: for the former case requires us to regard the self as divisible, whereas the latter does not. So on the ordinary naïve conception of the self we can understand why such a double success can be a failure: making two selves from the brain of one would have to be seen as the creation of totally new selves, whereas the preservation of a single hemisphere could assure the survival of the one old self. Having your brain divided would not, on the ordinary naïve conception, be as good as having your life span doubled, since these require quite different things of the nature of the self. According to the naïve conception, then, the self is so constituted that its survival cannot consist in anything other than its *identity* with a future self: this is because, not having self-like parts, it cannot continue to exist by virtue of division – identity is the only mode of survival for a simple substance.

It is tempting to infer from the foregoing discussion that cases of brain splitting and recombination may be dismissed as not showing what they are claimed to, namely, that there can be personal survival without identity. But, though we have brought forward reasons for doing this in a motivated way, we cannot really dismiss these cases as easily as that; for there is, it seems, no honest denying that brain division is not tantamount to total destruction. Even if you were intellectually persuaded by the previous discussion that the self cannot divide in the way the claim of survival without identity requires it to, you would probably still prefer brain division to death – despite your justified puzzlement as to *how* the self could survive in two or more parts. The truth of the matter seems to be that we are here confronted with a genuine antinomy: two sets of considerations about the self seem individually compelling, but they point to contradictory conclusions. What is significant is that the two sets of considerations issue from different ways of approaching the self – from the point of view of the ordinary psychological concept of the self, and from the point of view of the physical basis of the self. Viewed in this way the antinomy about the conditions of personal survival is a special case of the general problem (discussed in Chapter 2) of reconciling the content of our mental concepts with the fact of the physical involvements of the mental. The simplicity of the self is analogous in this respect to the subjectivity of sensations: our sensation concepts tell us that sensations are subjective in a way no merely physical state could be, yet we also believe that sensations must in some way depend upon physical properties of the brain – so we get a clash between two ways of thinking about sensations. Similarly, our concept of the self tells us it is a simple substance, but we also believe the self to depend upon the brain, which is a complex divisible substance: thought of mentally, the self cannot be divided, but when we think of it physically we seem compelled to suppose that this simplicity is in some way illusory. The choice therefore seems to be between deciding to ignore, however unreasonably, considerations drawn from the physical facts about the brain, on the one hand, and deciding to abandon or radically revise our conception of the self in the light of those facts, on the other. Neither decision can be taken in good conscience; so we are reduced to looking the antinomy in the face and despairing of a satisfying resolution. But there are occasions on which despair is to be preferred to concealing the troubling facts and so preventing full recognition of their import. The right response to brain fission and fusion cases, it would seem, is first to point out that the claim of survival without identity requires us to conceive the self in a way we in fact do not and whose coherence is dubious; then to acknowledge the force of the cases that have these rebarbative implications, thus admitting an antinomy in our ways of thinking about the self; and to diagnose the antinomy as arising from the difficulty of co-ordinating the distinctive character of the mind with the fact of its physical involvements, withholding final judgement pending some resolution of that general problem.

The conception of the self that has seemed to elude explanation in other terms was the naïve notion we are naturally prone to operate with. It may be that this notion is not, after all, coherent; but it is the notion we have, and any philosophical account of the self has as its first duty the elucidation of that notion. The onus is then on an opponent of the naïve notion to show it to be unacceptable. The ordinary conception of the self seems to credit it with the following (interrelated) properties: that it is a simple indivisible substance; that it is not ontologically reducible to other sorts of entities and their relations; that its presence is all-or-nothing; that its survival can consist in nothing other than its identity over time; that its survival is not a matter of degree (since it is simple in nature); that it is a mental concept whose essence is best revealed from the first-person perspective (it is to be seen first and foremost as the reference of 'I'); that its identity over time cannot be given non-trivial criteria. These properties are connected in various ways; but the fundamental property of the self, which underlies and explains the others, is the property of being a simple substance apprehended as such in self-consciousness. This explains why the self is irreducible and why we cannot give informative criteria of identity for it, and also why it seems that any future person is either definitely you or definitely not – why there cannot really be partial survival of a self. But it is a further question whether there is in the world any entity which meets these specifications, metaphysically stringent as they are. The concept of the self might, for all we have said, be in the same case as the concept of free will has often been supposed to be: we use the idea of freedom in application to the decisions and actions of people, but, in so far as we can make intelligible to ourselves what the concept demands, it can seem that no event in the natural world could be free – nothing could *count* as a free decision or action. Thus it might be said that just as the notion of pure spontaneity demanded by the idea of free will has no fulfilment in the world, so similarly the conception of the self as a simple substance with the properties cited cannot be supposed to pick out any real thing. If such allegations of unreality were correct, then we should have to abandon the concepts of freedom and the self as we have them and attempt to fashion some more hygienic concepts to put in their place. But we should need to hear some very powerful arguments before we are convinced that these concepts are thus void of application; and, at least in the case of the self, such arguments have not, it seems fair to report, been forthcoming. The nearest thing to an argument for abandoning the naïve conception of the self stems from the considerations about brain division we grappled with above; but the diagnosis we gave of those considerations should make us cautious about recklessly throwing over such a pervasive and important notion as that of the self. Short of a direct demonstration of incoherence in the naïve conception of the self, we therefore seem entitled – or perhaps driven – to the conclusion that the self should be conceived as a simple mental substance whose identity over time is primitive and irreducible.

Epilogue: The place of the philosophy of mind

No study of the philosophy of mind would be complete without some indication of the relationship between the philosophy of mind and other areas of philosophy. Briefly, then, we shall point to some relations of dependence between the investigation of the nature of mind and certain other philosophical questions. We shall find that the philosophy of mind occupies a position of centrality within philosophy as a whole: it is not just one department of the subject in which philosophical methods are brought to bear upon a particular topic – namely the mind – in the way that philosophy of morals, law, history, religion, mathematics, science and so on are appropriately so viewed; rather, it belongs with the more basic parts of philosophy – with epistemology, metaphysics and (in the opinion of some) philosophy of language. This is not (or not just) because some of the traditionally central questions of philosophy *are* issues in the philosophy of mind – the mind–body problem, the nature of the self, the relation between mind and reality; nor is it that in order to discuss the mind we need to take a stand on issues seemingly unrelated to it – for instance, causality, identity, meaning: there are these reasons, but there are more specific and less obvious ways in which the study of mind is deeply embedded in philosophy as a whole.

One way in which the philosophy of mind can be of especial significance has been alluded to earlier (Chapter 4): this is that philosophy is very much concerned with the structure and content of our *thought* about the world, and the nature of thought is a topic within the philosophy of mind. To know how we in fact represent the world, and the sorts of condition governing how we can represent it, is to know something about the world, as reflected in the concepts through which we apprehend it. Thus philosophers have very often put forward a certain theory of thought and proceeded to judge the credentials of various concepts according to whether they conform to the chosen theory of thought: if they fail to conform, they have been declared void of significance, with consequent revisions in our conception of the world. It is sometimes said that philosophy, or at any rate twentieth-century analytical philosophy, is primarily concerned with language and linguistic meaning. This is not false, but it needs to be put in proper perspective. Those who recommend a fundamental concern with language do so because they regard language as the royal road to thought: to investigate a concept we must investigate the words in the use of which that concept is exercised; so thought is still the intended object of study, though it is to be approached with a certain indirectness. The necessity for such indirectness can take a weak or a strong form. The weak thesis of the methodological primacy of language asserts that it is heuristically convenient to attend to the linguistic embodiment of concepts in investigating their content; it is not suggested that there is no sense in the idea of investigating concepts without doing so through language. The strong thesis claims that there is no separating thought from language, that thought necessarily has a linguistic vehicle; to investigate a concept just *is* to investigate words and their meaning – so there is no real indirectness. To maintain this strong thesis of the methodological primacy of language it is necessary to defend a certain view of the relation between thought and language – and to undertake such a defence is to place oneself within the territory marked out by the philosophy of mind. So in order to show that language is strongly fundamental in philosophy we would need to establish a thesis in the philosophy of mind, the thesis, namely, that thought requires language. The linguistic philosopher might want to claim that *this* thesis cannot be evaluated without recourse to language – specifically, to the meaning of mental words – but to claim this is really to assume what he has undertaken to establish. At the least we can say that considerations in the philosophy of mind, whether or not these are couched in terms of mental language, are needed to settle the question whether concepts may be investigated directly or only as expressed in words. But even if the linguistic philosopher could establish his strong thesis about thought, it would still be true that thought is where his real interest lies.

The project of devising a general theory of *meaning* as a way of coming at the problems of philosophy has its rationale, then, in the thesis that thought is essentially linguistic: this thesis is what lies behind the idea that a general theory of the content of thoughts must take the form of a theory of the meaning of sentences. But suppose we decided that thoughts were not essentially linguistic: then it would no longer seem right to take a general theory of meaning to be what will put philosophy on the path to the solution of its problems; we shall seek instead a general theory of the content of thoughts – this being a task for the philosophy of mind. Our proper procedure, on this supposition, would be to try to elicit the general principles which govern the way thought acquires its content, and the ways this content gets manifested in judgement and action. We would need to ask what central concept (if any) best elucidates the content of thought; whether we can develop a properly systematic theory of thought; whether it is possible to give a reductive analysis of what it is for a thought to be directed on to a proposition. Thus on the supposition that thought does not require a linguistic medium and so is not to be explained in terms of meaning, the philosophy of mind would be methodologically anterior to the philosophy of language – because concepts would be capable of direct investigation. Let us not now commit ourselves on the correctness of this conception of the relation between philosophy of mind and philosophy of language with respect to philosophy at large; it is enough to indicate the nature of the issue and the considerations needed to resolve it.

There is another, rather different, way in which the study of mind can prove important, even decisive, in the settlement of issues seemingly at some distance from the philosophy of mind. The question how the mind is constituted connects with issues about the nature of the relationship between mind and reality: our metaphysical view of some part of reality can require us to adopt a particular conception of the mind, and metaphysical views are answerable to considerations regarding the plausibility of the picture of mind they require. We can thus find ourselves enriching our picture of mind as a result of commitment to certain metaphysical views, or we can find, instead, that our prior picture of the mind forces us to revise our metaphysical views. Three examples of this sort of interplay between philosophy of mind and other disciplines may be mentioned: the question of non-natural mental powers; the question of innateness; and the question of objectivity. We cannot, of course, hope to treat fully of these questions here; we can only sketch their bearing upon the study of mind.

The question of non-natural mental powers arises in connection with the subjects of mathematics, logical necessity, and ethics (and others). Suppose we favour, on metaphysical grounds, accounts of these subjects which locate the corresponding facts outside the ordinary empirical world: numbers exist outside space and time; necessity involves facts transcending the actual world; ethical statements speak of values imperceptible to the senses. Then the question arises how the mind relates to facts so construed: in particular, how do we come to know about facts of these non-empirical sorts? It does not seem that our ordinary perceptual faculties will avail us in these cases, limited as they are to the concrete and causal; so we seem required to postulate special non-natural mental faculties capable of getting us into cognitive contact with the kinds of reality assumed by our metaphysics. The knowing mind thus begins to look richer and stranger than we had supposed, in proportion as the world to which it is directed is made to look richer and stranger. We can react to this sort of result either by repudiating the metaphysics that gave rise to it, feeling that the mind cannot be plausibly credited with such non-natural powers; or we can swallow the consequences and admit that the mind is other and stranger than we had supposed. What is plain is that the metaphysical doctrines in question cannot be adequately assessed independently of the philosophy of mind they entail. The general structure of the issue is this: an acceptable metaphysics must yield a credible epistemology; but an epistemology can be judged credible or incredible only with reference to the conception of the epistemic subject it presupposes; so metaphysics becomes answerable to the philosophy of mind. Conversely, we may put forward a philosophy of mind which conceives the mind to be possessed of certain cognitive powers, and then find that we cannot square this theory of mind with the metaphysics we independently accept. In these ways metaphysics and philosophy of mind are interdependent disciplines: the question of naturalism about the world and naturalism about the mind go hand in hand.

The question as to how the mind is innately constituted arises as follows: suppose we find that the mind is possessed of cognitive structures which are not presented in experience, so that these structures could not have been acquired simply by attention to what has been given in experience during the course of learning. Then there is the question what other origin these mental contents might have; and it has been suggested, early and late, that we must assume the mind to be innately endowed with various sorts of cognitive principles and capacities – indeed, that *knowledge* of certain propositions is built into our genes. This has been held of mathematics and grammar, among other things: the mind is not originally, on these views, intrinsically unstructured, an empty receptacle waiting to be filled by experience; it is, rather, natively shaped by principles and capacities which make knowledge of mathematics and grammar possible. The general structure of the underlying reasoning here is this: the mind has contents which cannot be explained in terms of the information that has been fed into it; but these contents must come from somewhere; so let us say that they were present innately. Here a particular view of the mind is determined by a claim about the character of mathematics or grammar, namely that their principles are not extractable from experience; and there is an interplay between the acceptability of this claim and the plausibility of the view of mind to which it leads – the issues cannot be

independently decided. As with the question about non-natural powers, the view we take of the nature of the reality on to which the mind is
directed is critical in arriving at a theory of mind – and contrariwise.

The third example of the role of the philosophy of mind in settling
broader philosophical questions concerns the endeavour to trace the
boundary between what is subjective and what is objective: that is, the
attempt to distinguish between those aspects of our view of the world
which reflect how the world is in itself independently of us and our
subjective peculiarities, and those aspects which have their basis in our
subjective constitution. Our view of the world evidently results from
the joint contribution of what is objectively present in it and our own
mental make-up; and it is an important philosophical task to determine where one contribution stops and the other starts – to determine
what is really 'out there' as distinct from what is merely projected by
us. This kind of question has arisen about many kinds of concept –
concepts of ethics and aesthetics, of necessity and probability, of time
and space, of colours and sounds, and doubtless others. The question
is always whether these are to be found in the mind-independent
world, and so would form part of an ideally objective description of
reality, or whether they reflect subjective elements which we are
mistakenly prone to attribute to things outside us. It is clear that such
issues have implications for the question how the mind is constituted,
and that their resolution must depend upon some theory of the mind
and its contribution to our view of the world. If you are a philosopher
who prefers to regard the concepts in question as picking out objective
traits of reality, then you will picture the mind as a passive mirror of
the world, not as a force that shapes the way the world presents itself to
us; but if you are disposed to hold that these alleged traits are merely
subjective projections, then you will have to assign a richer contribution to the mind – what the mind projects outward must come from its
intrinsic constitution. The mind will be perceived as more richly
endowed in proportion as the world is regarded as objectively impov-
erished. And again, particular views about what is objective need to be
assessed with reference to the conception of mind they lead to: a
feature can be denied objectivity only if our theory of the mind allows
us to locate that feature in the mind, and a feature can be declared
objective only if our theory of the mind does not require us to assign
that feature to it. In particular, if a feature is claimed to be subjective
the question must always arise as to *why* the mind is so constituted as to
harbour that feature. This sort of issue engages with deep (or at least
large) questions about how we should conceive the representational
powers of the mind: should we conceive of the mind of man as we tend

to conceive of the mind of God, as an ideal and disinterested reflector of all that is objectively real and of nothing else; or should we think of the mind in a more naturalistic way, as a useful organ of survival thrown up by natural selection, whose function is to serve the needs of the animal bearing it, and whose powers of objectivity and intelligence are rigidly determined by its evolutionary function? These two views of the mind will affect our attitude to such questions as whether we should expect objective reality to be inherently intelligible to us, and whether we can ever hope to know reality as it is in itself: these heady questions call for a theory of the mind that permits them to receive rational answers.

It would be misguided to infer from the points we have been making that the philosophy of mind is the most basic area of philosophy: probably no part of philosophy can claim that title (except, though trivially, metaphysics). But it would not be an exaggeration to claim that issues in the philosophy of mind lie at the heart of almost every philosophical question, and that no progress can be made on the central problems of philosophy without due consideration being given to the questions about mind that inevitably arise. This is true of both epistemology and philosophy of language, areas which have, at different times, been proclaimed fundamental to philosophy in general. Perhaps this is not very surprising in view of the fact that so much of philosophy is concerned with understanding the relation between mind and reality.

Further reading

The items cited below comprise those works that have particularly influenced the chapters of this book; it is not intended that these be taken as exhausting all that is meritorious (still less relevant) in writings on the topics in question. For a useful and up-to-date collection of works on the philosophy of mind, see N. Block, *Readings in the Philosophy of Psychology*, 2 vols. (Cambridge, Massachusetts: Harvard University Press, 1980).

Chapter 1

Aristotle, *De anima*, in *The Works of Aristotle*, Vol. III, ed. W. D. Ross (Oxford: Clarendon Press, 1931).

P. F. Strawson, *Individuals* (London: Methuen, 1959), esp. chap. 3.

L. Wittgenstein, *Philosophical Investigations* (Oxford: Blackwell, 1953); published in the United States by Macmillan, 1973.

Chapter 2

D. Armstrong, *A Materialist Theory of the Mind* (London: Routledge & Kegan Paul, 1968); published in the United States by Humanities Press, 1968.

D. Davidson, 'Mental Events' and 'The Material Mind', in *Essays on Actions and Events* (Oxford: Clarendon Press, 1980).

S. Kripke, *Naming and Necessity* (Oxford: Basil Blackwell, 1980), Lecture III; published in the United States by Harvard University Press, 1980.

T. Nagel, 'What is it Like to be a Bat?' and 'Panpsychism', in *Mortal Questions* (Cambridge: Cambridge University Press, 1979).

H. Putnam, *Mind, Language and Reality* (Cambridge: Cambridge University Press, 1975).

Chapter 3

P. T. Geach, *Mental Acts* (London: Routledge & Kegan Paul, 1957).

B. Russell, *The Problems of Philosophy* (Oxford: Oxford University Press, 1968; first published 1912), esp. chap. 5.

Chapter 4

D. Davidson, 'Thought and Talk', in *Mind and Language*, ed. S. Guttenplan (Oxford: Clarendon Press, 1975).

J. Fodor, *The Language of Thought* (Hassocks: Harvester Press, 1976); published in the United States by Harvard University Press, 1979.

P. T. Geach, *Mental Acts*, op. cit.

G. Harman, *Thought* (Princeton: Princeton University Press, 1973).

Chapter 5

D. Davidson, *Essays on Actions and Events*, op. cit.

B. O'Shaughnessy, *The Will: A Dual Aspect Theory* (Cambridge: Cambridge University Press, 1981).

Chapter 6

T. Nagel, 'Subjective and Objective', in *Mortal Questions*, op. cit.

D. Parfit, 'Personal Identity', in *Philosophy of Mind*, ed. J. Glover (Oxford: Oxford University Press, 1978).

J. Perry, *Personal Identity* (Berkeley: University of California Press, 1975).

S. Shoemaker, *Self-Knowledge and Self-Identity* (Ithaca: Cornell University Press, 1963).

B. Williams, *Problems of the Self* (Cambridge: Cambridge University Press, 1973).

Chapter 7

N. Chomsky, *Rules and Representations* (New York: Columbia University Press, 1980).

M. Dummett, 'Can Analytical Philosophy be Systematic, and Ought it to be?', in *Truth and Other Enigmas* (London: Duckworth, 1978); published in the United States by Harvard University Press, 1978.

Index

More OPUS books

The Standing of Psychoanalysis
B. A. Farrell

This book is a study of the two central problems raised by that notoriously controversial and confusing subject, psychoanalysis: how believable is it as a doctrine, and how effective is it as a therapy? In his account of the achievements of psychoanalysis, B. A. Farrell examines the nature of the support for the doctrine from case material, the validity of the psychoanalytic method as a tool of enquiry, and the results of scientific studies of the subject; he investigates the debate about the therapeutic effectiveness of psychoanalysis, and considers its relationship to history, psychiatry, objective psychology, and common sense. By clarifying the controversy which surrounds the subject, he dispels some of the confusions which perplex both expert and layman.

'Farrell has done very well indeed in the task he set himself, to examine psychoanalytic theory, and I learnt a lot from him.' Peter Medawar, *Sunday Times*

'obviously open-minded and sensible' H. J. Eysenck

'Brian Farrell has consolidated his long-standing interest in the logical and scientific status of psychoanalysis into a beautifully measured volume.' *Encounter*

'this is a challenging book to read, and provides endless points for discussion' *Mind Out*

A Historical Introduction to the Philosophy of Science
Second Edition

John Losee

Since the time of Plato and Aristotle, scientists and philosophers have raised questions about the proper evaluation of scientific interpretations. John Losee's book is an exposition of positions that have been held on issues such as the distinction between scientific enquiry and other types of interpretation; the relationship between theories and observation reports; the evaluation of competing theories; and the nature of progress in science. Professor Losee makes the philosophy of science accessible to readers who do not have extensive knowledge of formal logic or the history of the several sciences.

Structuralism and Since
From Lévi Strauss to Derrida
Edited by John Sturrock

France is never without one or more *maîtres à penser* – those charismatic, difficult thinkers whose ideas we see as giving permanent shape to a particular intellectual epoch. Claude Lévi Strauss, Roland Barthes, Michel Foucault, Jacques Lacan and Jacques Derrida are such figures: writers who, in their different disciplines, have made structuralism into the force that it is today. This book elucidates the structuralist phenomenon by considering the work of these five important thinkers, and aims to establish what is of lasting worth and originality in their work. It is a reasoned and positive presentation of an important body of contemporary thought.

'John Sturrock's . . . book is the best guide to its subject that has yet appeared . . . Brilliantly expounded, with cracking pace and unflappable self-confidence, the book is a mine of information and an indispensable primer to anyone who comes to the subject fresh and ready to make a new conquest.'
London Review of Books